BARBARIANS
AND
Beautiful Souls

The Dangerous Normalcy of
ORGANIZATIONAL BEHAVIOR

JEFFREY T. SACCHET

outskirts
press

TABLE OF CONTENTS

PREFACE

What qualifies me to write a book about human behavior as we experience it through the lens of the workplace?

I am not a medical doctor. I don't have a Ph.D. or a degree in industrial psychology. What I offer is a lifetime of invaluable lessons learned from years managing competitive teams. It is in the business of social capital and under the most demanding conditions where we see the best and worst of people. Sometimes leaders emerge. And sometimes, *barbarians* materialize with their neuroses, sociopathic behaviors, paranoia, and raging insecurities. Therefore, it was appropriate that I applied my efforts toward comprehending workplace behavior through the prism of my industry—luxury hospitality. It is a business with persistently complicated characters and unique challenges. Some say it is the perfect breeding ground for unpredictable behavior because of its high pressure, stress, and disproportionate rate of failure.

I have spent a substantial part of the last twenty years studying the behaviors, actions, and practices of people, what they disclose, and what they leave behind. By learning their motivators, and what shapes their attitudes, opinions, beliefs, reactions, and tolerances, I became more acutely aware of the nuances and deficiencies of my behavior. Eventually, I was able to cast aside the stories I had been telling myself, and I came to an awakening—a place so much more authentic and real.

It left me with an intense desire to understand the driving forces of social interaction better. I was set on a path to look more closely at seemingly routine exchanges among people and how trust relationships and alliances are formed or broken within the thinnest slices of life. I began to see human actions and reactions from a broader perspective.

I also learned how life's trajectory could be altered or determined by how successfully we manage just a few of life's opportunities. Our career paths and experiences are influenced in meaningful ways by the words, deeds, and actions of others we see and meet every day. People leave indelible tracks, and we take what we must from each. They can leave us with lessons of enlightenment or confounding, head-shaking moments of disillusionment.

Career successes and disappointments have significantly shaped my identity and sense of personal acceptance. My episode of instability, professional and otherwise, was a period of substantial loss—loss of opportunity, recognition, personal validation, and time. Perhaps, the highest price to pay is the loss of time. If we lose money, we go back to work. If we fail at love, we can still love, and perhaps enjoy relationships as if we weren't hurt. If dreams shatter, there is another. But time lost is life itself abandoned—enrichment, experience, and enjoyment forsaken.

Memories live within the framework of time. Our consciousness contains the uniqueness of our life story. Although to grasp this history, our mind must assign life events to specific moments in time. For example, "Where were you when…" and so on.

Time and opportunity are interrelated. Opportunity, either won or lost, organizes time into memory folders. If we win, it is considered time well spent, a good memory to be stowed away, and savored. If we fail, it is the advance of time we wish to suspend, a desire to replay life, and to bring back time, and relive the painful memory with an alternate outcome. The human brain is both the repository and the regulator of this process. Victims of a tragic car accident, for example, describe events unfolding in slow motion. It is the mind's way of arresting precious time, forestalling the inevitable while searching for a reset switch.

We measure success by the amount of time given to us. We evaluate failure by the time taken from us. In the end, we spend too much time contemplating events over which we have no control, like the painful loss of what could, or should, have been.

We take so many social interactions for granted. We are wired for psychological safety and the survival of our ego while we live and transact at the moment. We move through life routinely and within our carefully constructed force field. Along the way, we miss opportunities to make someone's day or to assign value and meaning beyond the immediate and apparent manifestations of ordinary circumstances.

With the average American working fifty or more hours per week, it is where we spend most of our waking hours. Within these hours, we demonstrate our best, and sometimes our worst, character qualities to the world. These are the behaviors people use to define us since most of our industry colleagues never see us display our at-home persona. It is, therefore, the workplace identity that precedes us. Not only is it usually the second question asked during an introduction, but it is also how acquaintances come to know us—Joseph the mechanic, Mary the attorney, and so on.

This work took two years to assemble, although its lessons were formulated throughout a lifetime. It lies at the intersection of human behavior, managing emotions, and our search for self-enrichment through stronger relationships.

We rarely know what lies inside of people. This book is my humble attempt to learn more about them.

These are some of their stories and mine.

INTRODUCTION

This book is not about leadership. There are many others for that purpose. However, it is a book about the underpins of effective leadership, which are the adaptive, prerequisite social behaviors for the responsible management of business relationships.

Actions flow from thoughts. We know the foundation of real and honest connection by identifying key thought drivers and our emotional flashpoints. If we study the shortcomings and life circumstances of others, we acquire a healthier understanding of our imperfections. In doing so, we gain a sharper awareness of humanity. It is also true in reverse. The more we know ourselves, able to identify our vulnerabilities and deficiencies better, the more we discover a broader appreciation for the needs of others.

At its center, it is a book about character and how we operate in the world. It looks at the people who helped shape my values and viewpoints through their personalities and dispositions. It is not a memoir, but rather a roadmap, presented in a series of case studies, to a more meaningful comprehension of our collective spiritual requirements.

All business is emotional. Emotion energizes workplace behavior. It underscores how we persuade, interact, form alliances, build trust, shape consensus, evaluate talent, and react to either success or failure. However, it is the responsible control of emotion that largely determines how we successfully navigate the complicated network of business relationships.

Therefore, this is a book of stories that attempts to get rational about the emotions we experience—anger, fear, anxiety, jealousy, empathy, suffering, and joy. It is also a book of anecdotes, awakenings, musings, and remembrances of both ordinary and compelling people with extraordinary character traits, and some with alarming behavioral liabilities. There are those with unflattering qualities—unpleasant attributes I have chosen to disconnect from my value system. These are selfish individuals who could never be vulnerable enough to lead with an open heart or an open mind. Blissfully unaware of how they appear to others, they are the barbarians in our midst. It is they who take a piece of us. They take our restful sleep, our esteem, pride, joy, and perhaps, our love of life.

It is a book of paradoxes. It is about disagreeable behavior that reveals what not to do so we can precisely know what we should do. We learn what not to do by witnessing the fallout from others' negative actions. This is the theory of anti-modeling—a dominant theme throughout this book.

Unfortunately, barbarian behavior is normalized—perhaps dangerously, through its acceptance by regular people—good, honest people—who, depending on the situation, are either enablers, witnesses, or possibly, victims of the circumstances. Whichever they are, they are all seekers of a lifeline, just ordinary coworkers looking to survive and protect themselves because the alternative is uncomfortable.

It is too simplistic to consider that those who occupy many cubicles and offices in our places of business are inherently inhumane. These are our pleasant next-door neighbors, the Sunday church visitors, the morning joggers, the dog walkers, and the mild-mannered relatives. No one dreams of becoming a barbarian; it is not an objective. It is a result. People do not become unpopular because of a lack of skill. They become detestable because of the mismanagement of their ego, or their lack of character.

I do not believe there are legions of evil associates, Machiavellians, artfully scheming, conniving, and bullying, as they cut vast swaths of devious, self-centered dishonesty. The very idea suggests that many of our closest team members are incorrigibly beyond restoration. However, there are unmindful people, both the powerful and the powerless, who are unaware of how their words and actions are filtered and interpreted by others. It is the authority figures, though, from whom we expect more. They who command and control are uniquely positioned to either exercise dominion by exploiting a power gap or providing psychological safety.

Then some straddle the line between benign mentor and harsh tormentor. It is they, the multi-dimensional beings, that are the most confounding because they stretch behavioral boundaries to either side of the spectrum. Even then, we may find something, one characteristic in them, to admire and respect.

Also, interspersed throughout this book are love letters or the stories of *beautiful souls*. They lived in a way where insight that could have led to healing or transformation was out of reach. Indeed, every love story has so much more—hope, loss, frustration, yearning, conflict, and mortality. Sometimes our most valuable findings are from examples of catastrophe and redemption. I have learned from them because their stories tug on different heartstrings. They help build our emotional toolkits. They provide the gift of perspective and are vivid reminders that even during times of ruin, the vestiges of humanity and compassion are there to keep us whole.

It would be a mistake to exclude from this work examples of the devastating effects of mental insufficiency. Some argue it is a burden on my industry that is reaching epidemic proportions. The sector suffers from disproportionate levels of substance abuse. Those who seek relief through self-medication often have an underlying psychological disorder due to their inability to appropriately manage the forces of life.

The industry is a magnet for workers who can rewrite their history and start anew merely by walking into a restaurant up the street. Aside from a few perfunctory questions about relevant experience, they can pick up an apron and hit a reset switch because verification of their employment record is usually pointless. Perhaps it is another illustration of paradox that an industry which thrives on delivering comfort, relaxation, and respite is often unable to take care of its most significant asset—its people. Conversely, the same people who are unable to take care of themselves manage to take care of millions of others successfully.

This work began as a business book. And from a learning point of view, it still is, told through a lens of personal experiences. It became for me, in a greater context, one flawed man's journey to a more meaningful acceptance of the human condition with all its wonderment, faults, and frailty.

Acceptance is authenticity. By recognizing what we cannot control or change, we realize we are all there is to change. We can adjust our reactions to the emotional triggers threatening to obfuscate the character traits we want the world to see. We then arrive at a place of tolerance and transparency, free of anger, frustration, and recrimination. Once we manage emotion through knowledge and awareness, we become the genuine and dependable coworkers we want to be.

We see people—from the barbarians to the beautiful souls and all those in between. They are the heroes, the optimists, the cheerful, and the pure. They are the hopeless dreamers, the dream makers, the addicted, the anxious, the depressed, the ordinary, and extraordinary. They walk among us and talk and interact with us. They work, go home, and live their lives. They don't always know themselves. Still, we know them. We are them. And they are dangerously normal.

This book is for you and for them too. May they find their way in life and business, wherever they may go. Through the lessons I have learned, I would like to show you, and them, how.

Come with me.

Chapter 1

———— ❧ ————

RALPH AND COLORFUL
CHARACTERS IN CRAZY PLACES

"Blessed are the weird people—poets, misfits, writers, mystics, painters and troubadours—for they teach us to see the world through different eyes."— Jacob Nordby

THE CHARACTERS, THE colorful cast of crazy, zany, wild, wonderful, and beautiful oddities that occupy the halls of hospitality, come in all sizes, shapes, religions, and colors. They are the rainbow, same as they were long before we began using the term as a rallying cry for equality. They represent diversity now and have since before we came to know diversity, which is part of company orientation programs across the business landscape.

In many instances, their history, life choices, or level of formal education doesn't qualify or suit them for the nine-to-five environment. Sometimes they are outcasts from that world, proudly wired differently than the professional office inhabitants employed by banks, insurance companies, law firms, publishing houses, advertising agencies, and public relations firms.

Not content with life in a cubicle, they are the grinders, the creatures of the night, the denizens of the dark, and the working wounded. They are the weekend warriors who work so others can play. They are the students paying tuition, the single moms with kids to feed, and the grandma without kids to feed. They are the realtors trying to sell a house by the day and waiting tables at night to make ends meet. They are the moonlighting cops, the disabled veterans, the college rejects, and the servers who want to be movie stars. They are the teachers who can't survive on public school pay and the alcoholics who can't keep a job.

To this lively cast, I owe a debt of gratitude. They provide education and worldliness that are in equal measures hilarious and enlightening, a learning experience unavailable at an expensive university. The service industry harvests people such as these. Its survival is dependent on a colorful cast of individuals we ask to be confident, self-reliant, adaptable, dependable, and honest in the face of chaotic conditions that change at a dizzying pace.

Unlike the nine-to-five private sector, the entry barriers to this club—the unofficial fraternity of hospitality workers—are lower by design and necessity. A qualified restaurant server, for example, doesn't need a specialized degree of higher education or specific knowledge within an academic discipline. In most cases, their job requirements are limited to having a pleasing personality, physical dexterity, and some previous, and, hopefully, relevant experience.

Their motivations for employment are different than their office counterparts. Their needs are immediate, and their existence is more transient. The results of their efforts are instantaneous. Their value is determined each time they place a bill of fare in front of a diner. The corporate world determines individual self-worth by the dreaded annual review and a weekly paycheck. It is a slower grind with different rhythms, and a sense of gratification which increases incrementally, rarely exponentially, by an annual cost-of-living wage adjustment.

The inhabitants of the office share a different set of motivators. Usually, recipients of higher education, they begin with wide-eyed hopes and dreams. They occupy rungs on a ladder. Each level has its set of bosses, rules, and expectations. However, at its apex, the ladder has a broader set of standards, practices, and assumptions, sometimes called company culture. Each rung is an independent but connected subset of the ladder. Each is occupied by individuals whose conduct and attitudes contribute to the more significant manifestations and outward expressions of the company's philosophy. Culture is what the company presents to the public as its mission statement or reason for being.

Workers subscribe to a code of conduct and a set of objectives to reinforce the company's promise. The formula is simple. Exceed expectations and move up a level at a time. It is a time-tested methodology requiring all the inhabitants to share a standard set of values and ideals aligned with the mission statement. It is conformity at its most pure. Independent ideas and actions within the levels are encouraged, although individual authority is only valuable as a direct, contributing benefit to the advancement of the collective purpose.

There is a reason why we hear so few individuals experiencing a meteoric rise through the corporate ranks. The slower ascension implies and demands there be an investment in time, and in living the values. It is a dues-paying culture, with each day on the job growing interest. Hospitality workers, particularly wait staff, rarely make such an investment. With few exceptions, living within tightly prescribed work principles is secondary to their reason for being. It is a people business, a colorful entertainment business, and non-conformist behavior is almost encouraged in their environment.

We were a small clique of young waiters at an old restaurant of still-intact reputation in the 1970s—just sheltered middle-class kids navigating through the maze of early adulthood on the way to the coveted nine-to-five world. We were there because our parents couldn't provide the funds to send us to expensive institutions of higher learning. The immediate dollars paid school tuition and helped us obtain a sought-after first automobile, our rite of passage into adulthood. Having a car at age seventeen meant independence and a more vibrant social life.

The restaurant, a quirky one still in good standing, was on an eclectic little island, a small, blue-collar community with a population of five thousand set on two hundred fifty acres. Its only connection to the rest of the city was a two-lane bridge. There was only one way in and one way out, unless by boat. From a socio-cultural perspective, the little bridge may have been twenty miles long and a mile high.

The place was an attraction for tourists with its many restaurants, tee-shirt shops, and mom-and-pop stores, which could only exist on their haul from the busy season, May through September. But the island was, in fact, a destination. Laid back, and surrounded by gentle waters, its visitor population exploded in summer and on weekends. For many inner-city residents, it was a temporary respite from the usual brick-and-mortar existence of closed-in urban quarters and sweltering summer heat that radiated off the hot asphalt.

The community was a physical and cultural peculiarity. Ramshackle and battered by salt air, the nautical nature of the island was in stark contrast to the rest of the inner-city neighborhoods I knew. In this place, time seemed to stand still. Working-class families occupied the isle along with its brand of street toughs born and bred there. My sheltered young mind didn't comprehend the island mentality, and I never understood why the attraction of the week was the usual and customary bar brawl. These were small-town folks in a big city who usually made their own rules and resolved disputes with old-fashioned street justice.

As outsiders who came onto the island only to work, we were sometimes viewed with sideways glances. Part-time islanders, we didn't fit into the fabric of everyday life. We didn't support their stores, their schools, or their local economy. We were either viewed as carpetbaggers or interlopers. Sometimes both. Although for us, it was an opportunity wrapped in a tidy package. The restaurants needed us, and we needed them. It was a matter of reciprocity and survival.

He was about thirty-five years old, and I remember the first time I saw him. It was a sunny Sunday afternoon. His entrance to the restaurant mesmerized me. He was an unforgettable sight against the backdrop of the rough-and-tumbled surroundings of the little working-class island. He seemed completely comfortable in his skin. Light on his feet, he moved with a deliberation that radiated gracefulness and poise. With disarming soft eyes and his chin held high, he flashed a cherubic, carefree smile that immediately welcomed people into his orbit.

Gold adorned his neck, fingers, and wrists. He wore tailored shorts, flip-flops, and a tee-shirt emblazoned with the curious words, "So Many Men. So Little Time." An expensive leather overnight bag on his shoulder and a Hermes scarf draped gently around his neck completed the look. Costly Van Cleef & Arpels was his cologne of choice. He must have looked like a fish-out-of-water as he traveled the city's seedy public transit system on his way to work.

Ralph was a novelty to our little gang of naïve, like-minded co-workers. Nevertheless, he was a most pleasant, charming, gregarious man of unrepentant pride, and impeccable style. He was an essential ingredient in the jambalaya of independent personalities that made the tough work so entertaining and bearable.

It was an intense place, owned and managed by individuals who subscribed to the unenlightened leadership sensibilities of the day. However, Ralph was the flamboyant, witty, humorous, and refreshingly irreverent foil from among our merry melting pot of middle-class workers. He was a walking recorder of head-snapping, unconventional one-liners, side-splitting sound bites, and hilarious double entendres, which usually referenced his lifestyle. He laughed at himself, and he embraced the belief that he had one life to live, and his greatest obligation was to be true to himself and his loved ones.

We didn't know what to make of Ralph. He was a harmless soul whose outward manifestations didn't fit any predetermined stereotypes residing in our young and unsophisticated minds. He wore enough jewelry to make himself a spectacle while traveling through the city's rough tenderloin at all hours. He lived in the big city, and I was curious to meet anyone fortunate enough to reside in such a gilded place, a place that, to my young mind, was full of excitement and wonder.

He was a talker, so conversing with him felt comfortable and natural, and I was drawn to this charming and mysterious man who wore unusual tee-shirts. During one such conversation, the topic turned to relationships and marriage. Ralph told me he was married once for three years, and that was enough. He described his current partner in life, a successful stage actor who recently developed skin cancer.

A kindly man, Ralph sensed my confusion as I wondered about the nature of his first marriage. He took me aside, and in his broken Cubano-English, he explained that we all live under the same sun. We worship the same God. We take care of our families the same way. We have the same desire in life, which is to live grandly in the time we have. He said we have the same problems and the same disappointments. We love the same, although, for Ralph, it was love too, but in reverse—nothing better and nothing worse.

He tried to play the role of big brother by advising me with a cautionary tale that if I were going to survive relationships, I would have to learn to hold back fifteen percent in a personal, emotional slush fund. He said that I should love passionately, but always love as if I might be hurt. To my young mind, those were words to live by. He was still a man of peculiar bearing to me, but with his enormous heart in the right place, I chose to meet him exactly where he stood.

It was an odd circle of friends. Raised in the grittiness of our environment, we knew each other from mid-teens and united by common dysfunction. In time, the names and faces at the old place changed, but we remained constant as we worked our way through the school years. The restaurant provided enough cash for us to pay for an excellent university education. Along the way, we adopted Ralph into our little posse. So, there we were, a few city ruffians raised on asphalt—and Ralph.

Restaurant workers are notorious prowlers of the night. On many nights after a long shift, adrenaline flowed from five p.m. to eleven p.m., and we weren't ready to go home. So, we took Ralph with us. If anything, Ralph's love of life and playful recklessness made him infinitely adaptable to almost any social situation. Always a source of amusement and entertainment wherever he went, his easy-going, conversive nature made us all laugh a little heartier. He gleefully played the role of the square peg in a round hole, the wisecracking sidekick who was never at a loss for words.

When we graduated from college, it was also time to move on from the place that had more than served its purpose. As we proceeded on to adult life, and I to a grand hotel in the city's downtown, Ralph sensed it was also time to depart. Always a bit of a schemer, he conveniently forgot to return one credit card too many to unsuspecting diners and found himself under suspicion for fraud. After several cards were reported lost, investigators connected dots back to him after patrons pegged him as the offender. They came to question Ralph once they discovered dubious purchases of jewelry, perfume, and expensive Champagne connected to the missing cards.

Still, Ralph was a wily industry veteran, and he learned a few tricks along the way. Undaunted by authoritative-looking men with suspicion on their minds, Ralph was a step ahead of them as he suddenly forgot the English language. Almost on cue, he feigned ignorance while swooning with incredulity. In the end, the merchant was paid, and the only victim was the behemoth credit card company, which for Ralph was the same as a victimless crime.

Later, he came to visit me at that grand hotel. He introduced me to his partner, the gentleman he told me about earlier who developed skin cancer. It was now 1984, and HIV was beginning to dot the landscape, eventually claiming the lives of thousands of men. In the big city, it was particularly virulent. The skin cancer Ralph had described to me was later known as Kaposi's Sarcoma, a form of cancer prevalent among people with AIDS. Ralph's partner died shortly after that. Several years later, Ralph declined. Distraught over his health, yet still passionately proud, he tried to keep his illness a private affair. For a man who lived so fiercely and resolutely, he never wanted to be a burden. He quietly slipped away in 1991.

I know that had he not suffered an untimely and horrific death, we would have found him when social media opened the vault to friends and acquaintances of the past. I also know he would still be doing what he always did—laughing, loving, and celebrating life unashamedly, proudly, and without regret. In his way, he was one of the most daring men I have known. To live the way he lived, at the time he lived, was nothing short of extraordinary. And there he was in his tee-shirt, proudly inviting anyone to deny him his obligation to be true to himself while he lived and loved in reverse.

Many years later, I think of what he told me. I wonder about the fifteen percent he fiercely held onto that was supposed to save him from danger. For Ralph, eighty-five percent was good enough to live. Ironically, the fifteen percent he designed to protect him was also sufficient to hurt him in the worst imaginable way.

More than three decades later, our little group of friends is still active, although we are in different corners of the country. We try to see each other once a year. We laugh as we remember Ralph because there was hardly a moment when he wasn't laughing at himself. Now and then, I open an unexpected text message, and a soundbite lets me know someone from our group is thinking of him.

And that is the legacy he left behind. Perhaps it was an accidental legacy, one he would undoubtedly dismiss. He would laugh at the idea that he left behind anything of notable achievement. Although how do we assign meaning to the indelible recollections we have of this man or anyone whose memory, many years later, still resonates mightily within the recessed folders of our minds? We have our answer if we subscribe to the notion that legacy is the result of meaningfully connected remembrances and relationships. Legacy is like a child plucking pebbles from a sandy beach and saving them in a memory box until they eventually overflow. As they cascade, each bouncing stone is a reminder of an echo in time—a time recalled with joy, or perhaps, with a bittersweet sadness.

Of the many people who passed through the portals of our lives, he remains the one who lived as if he knew time was his most precious commodity.

In the end, that is what makes him unforgettable.

Chapter 2

A Queen and Her Lights

"It has always been the aim of royalty and aristocracy to lower the individual liberty and independence of the common people. A baron and a minute-man could not breathe the same air." — John Boyle O'Reilly

HER HOTEL KINGDOM was a place most fitting for royalty. It was a new property of AAA Five Diamond status, which meant the plating on the bathroom fixtures was a little shinier than the Four Diamond property down the street. Or perhaps the fringes on the Oriental rugs were combed a little straighter.

It was born in 1980, and it ran parallel with a time of mad excess, a wild Wall Street bull market, and the most conspicuous consumption the nation had ever known. In many ways, the 1980s was a transitional decade of turbulent shifts in job growth, wealth accumulation, and cultural change. It was a sudden reversal of the previous decade's economic suppression and austerity with fuel embargos, unsustainable interest rates, and runaway inflation. It signaled the death of the three-martini lunch era that gave way to a more responsible happy hour, which at least didn't begin until five p.m.

She exploded onto the scene during a time when hoteliers were invisible, stately gentlemen with recognizable brands. Their names were blue-chip marketing tools, which provided a stamp of quality approval on the marquis of a building. Their designations suggested familiarity and consistency of delivered goods and services. But she was different, and she turned the prototype of the successful hotelier on its head by staging a marketing coup, making herself the star of the show. She was the first hospitality celebrity long before reality TV cultivated such people.

She was probably everything anyone ever heard about her, and she ruled with an iron fist from manicured hands. She was an enigma—a complicated, complex, baffling paradox of regal entitlement, tyrannical behavior, business brilliance, profound crudeness, elegance, despicable saltiness, and charitable benevolence. She was a fascinating representation of an individual who was decades ahead of her time and an illustrative portrait of her time.

She thrived in an organizational model with a vast power differential between those at the crown of the prototype and those beneath. That disproportion provided a dispensation, a distinction in rights and privileges reserved for those at the very top, and she exploited the disparity with the triumphant air of disdainful superiority.

In 1983, I was greeted with the warning to engage the Queen at my peril since her stories of cruelty were legendary. The orientation I received from the company wasn't nearly as entertaining as the one I received from my new associates. The restaurant manager gleefully informed me she threw a dinner roll at him when the homemade dough concoction wasn't to her satisfaction. It didn't matter that he didn't bake the roll himself. Nevertheless, since it was his dining room, he took the bullet, or the roll, in the gut for the team. The room service manager related his experience of an occasion when she didn't like her usual tuna salad sandwich. She called him to her office and asked him to hold out his hand as she deconstructed the offensive sandwich. She then proceeded to slap his hand with the lettuce. It was insufficiently crisp and a little wet on the edges.

To survive an encounter with her involving a weapon of convenience was to wear a war wound proudly, a badge of honor. It was a time before glaring spotlights on boardroom behavior, and it wasn't suggested that her actions amounted to physical assault. Although not of a menacing variety, her weapons were whatever was within arm's reach: dinner rolls and Iceberg lettuce.

Consistent with sensibilities of the period, if those at the top of the organization presented a superior product to the public and satisfied their investors, their behavior and indiscretions usually remained unchallenged. Closeted secrets only added to their alluring mystery. Did she throw a roll? Or was it a butter knife? Or perhaps the salt and pepper shakers? Such stories took on a life of their own, becoming more colorful as they made their way through the ranks of curiously perplexed onlookers.

Surrounded by sycophants, she moved in an entourage of preening toadies, bodyguards, and members of curious media outlets who heard her behavior made for entertaining news. Other hangers-on could make cast-off money or feel good about themselves just by being in her orbit. The attraction certainly wasn't that they could spend an afternoon entranced by her wit and charm. On the contrary, they came to enjoy a spectacle, something to make them feel more alive—a story they could take home and retell with wide-eyed astonishment. Unfortunately, given the stage and the opportunity, she rarely disappointed them.

Perhaps if the sleep was right the night before, she could engage in cheerful banter, almost humanlike. She was also expert at reflexively flipping facial expressions on and off. She could flash a smile as quickly as she could turn down the corners of her mouth to form an anxiety-producing sneer. When it came, it was immediate, and an omen of worse things to come. What usually followed was a menacing tirade without proportion, or discretion. The sneer was just one weapon in an arsenal of many. Nevertheless, there was a greater fear of the weapons we were yet to see.

We could never prepare for what might follow should she arrive at the dining room. Before sitting for lunch, she could have the staff in an anxiety-induced frenzy, organizing their mental battle stations. The trigger could be a piece of cheese on display. For example, a cheeseboard with her name on it would never be disgraced by a most pedestrian Wisconsin Cheddar when a delicate, truffle-scented Brillat Savarin would do. In a perpetual game of "gotcha," she expected that others possess the same heightened sensibilities she had, whether she expressed them or not.

The dining room was a pink nightmare of her design, which was impossible to keep pristine. There is a saying that you plan something the way you wish to continue doing it. So, if you don't want to spend resources, time, and material on the perpetual maintenance of pink fabric, you don't use it at the start. But it didn't matter. If the fabric was stained, someone was in the line of fire. A pragmatic understanding that pink material would soil was not a consideration. Nevertheless, with her random notions disconnected from practical reality, common sense was rarely an available option.

On one occasion, she arrived at the dining room with the usual parade of followers. I was in the pantry when she walked in. She quizzically asked the usually rhetorical question. She designed it to spring a trap, to exert control for the theatrical benefit of her audience. "What's this?" as she pointed to a breadboard with crumbs on it, the residue from a hectic luncheon service. Not wanting to patronize her with the obvious answer that it was a breadboard, I asked how I could assist her. She said, "Let me show you how to keep a breadboard clean." She found a clean towel, then asked me to hold the towel so she could guide my hand, scrubbing out the corners of crumbs that populated the breadboard. With a measure of satisfaction, she said, "That's how you clean a breadboard."

She was on stage and in her element. Despite the crowd that formed and uncomfortably watched her performance, I allowed myself a degree of relief, knowing on one occasion, I was the recipient of her rare motherly attention. There was nothing to say to her, except, "Thank you." It was, perhaps, a sad testimonial to the environment she created. She reduced her employees to thank her for the occasions when she wasn't an unconscionable barbarian.

Barbarians are in the business of hegemony, and she had little regard for appearances. She didn't worry about them because she didn't have to. She moved effortlessly in a world without limitations, and she thrived, knowing others weren't free to be themselves in her presence. She insisted on being everyone's top priority, pushing buttons to provoke a reaction she could exploit as a weakness. Unable to temper her unreasonable expectations, she was under the power of her irrational need to control. Her sense of satisfaction came from knowing she could reduce other people's choices, forcing them to surrender to circumstances. It was her way of having command over reality, reinforcing in her mind that most people are unreliable, with an unexpressed or unrealized need to be controlled.

With her constant need for domination, we were never able to divine where her thoughts would take her. When we anticipate loathsome conduct, the typical reaction is to engage in preliminary damage control by formulating ideas and escape plans to remain ahead of inevitable conflict. Today, we refer to such preventative action as "managing the boss."

We could attempt to survive her, but not to manage her, since her gun was always pointed somewhere. She could walk into a room and ask, "What is wrong with the lights?" The assumption was the lights malfunctioned, and the people in charge of the room were incompetent or negligent, or perhaps they didn't have her keen sense of aesthetics, which to her mind was the same as incompetence. It was a classic entrapment, and she was a ruthless tactician.

For her, it was a zero-sum proposition. Either the lights worked to her eyes, or they didn't, and someone was to blame. When the question came about the offending lights, no one dared say, "I don't know," because that was the same as admitting gross ineptitude, confirming all her negative suspicions. We didn't say we already called the building engineer because she would have left her table to call him, wondering what was taking him so long to fix the alleged broken lights. Nevertheless, I was raised to be gritty when necessary. I would be ready on the next occasion with a one-size-fits-all reply to her interrogative query about the lights.

The wag of her finger came from table #7. I took a deep breath as adrenaline began to flow. With a little bounce in my step, I tried to project confidence and control. "What is wrong with the lights?" Feeling proud that I had a plan, I told her I recognized there was something wrong with the lights, and I was just about to call the building engineer. She couldn't say, therefore, that I was too ignorant to recognize the problem, and she couldn't know I didn't act to repair them.

I allowed myself a little smile. The Queen looked at me for a second, and then it came. "Don't double-talk me, son! What is wrong with the lights? *And if you don't know, then say you don't know.*" She knew I was tap dancing and seeking a safe place to land somewhere in the squishy, blameless middle. In other words, the answer that was acceptable to her was the one everyone feared the most. She wanted honesty. Defeated and deflated, I just slithered away. Little did I know, the lesson she was teaching was about integrity and accountability.

Like many with extraordinary entitlement, she had unreasonable expectations that revolved around her demands. So perhaps unsurprisingly, she succumbed to old-fashioned greed, moving money illegally like in a shell game. Eventually she was convicted of tax evasion in a media circus environment. She owed a nominal amount in comparison to other high-profile schemes. For years, she looked down on those who didn't have her wily intelligence, industriousness, or the inclination to accomplish what she achieved. That changed when the district attorney opened the door to her unsatiated self-indulgence. It was spectacular retribution for one of the city's most influential and recognizable businesspeople. Sentenced to a few years in prison, she served about twenty months.

Over the years, I saw her twice more. The sneer that made her intended targets recoil in fear was gone. A felon, she could no longer associate with a business enterprise with a liquor license. She lost all of it, and now she was completely disarmed. I don't believe she remembered me, and if she did, what was I to say to her? She smiled broadly, extended her hand, and said, "Hello. It's nice to see you." All I could say was, "Thank you. I am delighted you joined us."

She became like most grandmothers I know. As I watched this kindly, older woman enjoy a pleasurable ninety minutes without reporters, cameras, and hangers-on types, I searched my mind for what became of the tyrannical bullying and the unconscionable behavior. Now alone and vulnerable, I knew then that the worst of her appeared when she was in front of an audience that found her to be a curiosity, a complete American original—authentic, bold, and brassy.

Her audience may not have liked her, but they couldn't keep their eyes off her. She knew they came to see a drama unfold. And just as she refused to disappoint her hotel guests, she didn't dissatisfy her spectators either. She didn't care for their affection if she had their admiration. But now the show was over, the costume and mask removed, and the curtain closed. As I watched her that night, the words forgiveness and humility kept coming to my mind—forgiveness from me, and finally, humility for her.

If I could see her now, without a legacy or a trace of her name on a building or a hotel, I would want to know if it was all worth it. Her behavior notwithstanding, in her way, she was teaching, demanding we win as she won. What mattered were the results, the satisfaction of doing something to be great. Though her standards were ragingly high, she knew excellence wasn't an accident. It happened as a result of meticulous planning and the repetition of carefully scripted actions.

Even the episode with the lights had new meaning for me years later. It was never about the lights, or the pink fabric, or the stain on the carpet. It was about leadership and command. It was about standing tall and being fully accountable for what was in my charge. She knew that her success, our success, was about mastering nuances, the difference-makers hidden to those less aware. For her, there was a profound distinction between liking a product or loving a product. And that is why the story of lights still resonates.

Her downfall was more about her style and less about the relative weight of her crimes. It didn't help her that she moved through life so stridently. After many employees, the serfs of her fiefdom came forward with tales of horrific encounters with her; any jury would convict her based solely on her reputation as a micromanaging, mean-spirited human being.

I heard she died a reclusive and lonely woman. In the end, she failed to know her audience members. They weren't just the bemused onlookers in the expensive front row seats—the ones only there for the pageantry and the spectacle. They disappeared when the show closed. Those relationships were a mile wide, but an inch deep. The relationships that mattered were those she didn't have with people who were the trial's witnesses and a jury of her peers. They were the ordinary people in the balcony, on the periphery, and in the standing room only section.

During the trial, they let her know how she made them feel. They let her know we aren't here to accumulate power and wealth at the expense of other human beings. She was convicted because she forgot the priorities of life, and in the end, she became the peril of the legacy she thought she carefully created.

Chapter 3

WILLIAM THE ORIGINAL

"We are so accustomed to disguise ourselves to others that in the end we become disguised to ourselves." — *Francois de La Rochefoucauld*

□ Brilliant □ Boisterous □ Industrious □ Energetic □ Charismatic □ Competitive □ Spirited

□ Determined □ Resourceful □ Opinionated □ Persuasive □ Insightful □ Independent

□ Autonomous □ Abrasive □ Blunt □ Obsessive □ Opinionated □ Narcissistic □ Irrational

□ Impatient □ Haughty □ Meticulous □ Cantankerous □ Ambitious □ Abrupt □ Testy

□ Motivated □ Proud □ Visionary □ Loyal □ Discerning □ Compelling □ Erratic □ Accurate

□ Flamboyant □ Compulsive □ Conscientious □Extraverted □ Crude □ Zany □ Judgmental

□ Perceptive □ Intuitive □ Reliable □ Emotional □ Excitable □ Irritable □ Demonstrative

□ Methodical □ Reckless □ Stressed □ Annoyed □ Unconventional □ Impulsive □ Dutiful

□ Controlling □ Spontaneous □ Imaginative □ Diligent □ Aggressive □ Animated □ Vigorous

It Reads Like A Checklist for a personality assessment. William moved in a world of extremes, and he checked all the boxes. He was one of those individuals you meet, and you don't see them in any other role. Always impeccable in a navy-blue suit, he never gave the impression he had cut his teeth in the business as a busboy.

He was the only (tor)mentor I have known who could captivate a room while simultaneously insulting its occupants. Animated, boisterous, energetic, unashamed, rude, and crude, he could fill a room with boundless energy and make people explode in fits of laughter or recoil in fear from his searing invectives. However, they were rarely business-related insults. Instead, his arsenal's readymade weapons were his observations of body weight, gender, body shape, ethnicity, body parts, hairstyle, sexual orientation, and the like. None of it was off-limits.

He was a caricature of himself. People hung on his words to experience the guilty pleasure of hearing wild histrionics tumble from his unfiltered mind. His ability to cut through pretentiousness and haughtiness with rapier wit or a stinging slur made him a hero of idol worship to some and the devil to others. Completely comfortable in his role as the detestable skunk at a garden party, he was a living and breathing human resources nightmare. A prisoner of his personality, he never saw himself as a man whose behavior needed to be modified.

Still, he survived because company handbooks in the 1980s rarely included specific employee safeguard policies. Codified rules of personal behavior for senior managers were few and far between. It was also a time when staff members remained silent in the face of boorish and bullying behavior. It would take another twenty years and subsequent generations of employees to blur the lines between themselves and their rulers and to force the hand of companies and their senior leaders to become more transparent.

Most of us in William's charge were men and women in our twenties. We were single, unattached, and the beneficial recipients of the exciting social structure that an immense vertical hotel provided. Such properties are like little cities. You could visit something or somebody new almost every day. However, our jobs also offered the means to a competitive income and a clear career trajectory assisted by the cachet and pedigree of a prestigious brand.

The fringe benefit of social bonding created by the shared experience of surviving in a demanding industry only added to the attractiveness of our opportunity. We wrestled daily with almost impossible expectations in a setting fraught with emotions and human and mechanical fragility. William's behavior, or anyone else's, was secondary to the more significant task—the administration of the company business, and no one did it better than William. He was so efficient he could have asked for and probably received a license to steal. It was in this environment of relatively few boundaries where he was practically untouchable.

While perceptive women who crossed his path found William to be an oddity of maddening, chauvinistic excesses, it was the men who silently wanted to be like him. Effortlessly wielding leverage and power, the prestige of his appointment preceded him. Having been in his position for ten years, he survived all the other senior directors who came and went around him. He usually had a demeaning nickname for any of his equals that didn't have his energy or business sensibilities. Nevertheless, it was his business acumen and industriousness that set him apart. He was a friend to celebrities, religious deities, heads of state, politicians, dignitaries, and ambassadors. He made his work look exciting, and if it wasn't his chair we wished to sit in someday, it was another just like it somewhere else.

He could be dismissive, especially towards vocal and self-assured women. Their only sin was they were, perhaps, more confident than he was. He made sure they knew their place in his world. It took a poised, strong-willed woman to challenge William successfully. Only a few did and survived. He didn't appreciate women who questioned his motives or his authority. He was usually impatient with their drama over working conditions or alleged cruel treatment. It was easy for him to make them an offer to resign before he summarily fired them. Feeling powerless and with few alternatives, most departed silently, believing they were over-matched, and they were.

He could be extraordinarily flip, hilarious, and ragingly inconsiderate with his assistants. He expected that his beleaguered helpers understand his business needs, and he could be brazenly impertinent toward them. I remember walking into his office on several occasions and thinking he had some Svengali grip on them. William also knew what type of individual he could control with his brand of psychological dominance. He seemed to derive unique pleasure from pushing his limitations with them to evoke either laughter, shock, anger, disgust, or fear. But to William, it was all the same.

When I first met William, it was the year of a citywide hotel union worker's strike. With every hotel line staff employee in the city taking to the streets, we manned posts with a mix of recently recruited replacement workers of questionable skill and the hotel's managers. We made beds by morning and served guests in the dining rooms by night.

The Hotel Workers Union in most cities is a powerful entity. When we consider how much tourism moves through a major city, a work stoppage means thousands of hotel guests are without services. In a city with two hundred fifty hotels, a general strike can force as many as thirty-five thousand workers to the streets. Not content to be confined behind police barricades, the bedlam spilled to the avenues as workers ignored sensibilities of kindly behavior. They stomped and snaked through the city with strength-in-numbers impunity. They marched and snarled already strained traffic and chanted every day for weeks until they lost their voices. I recall the irony that these same employees, trained in the art of selfless service, could flip a switch, and behave so menacingly when bound by a common purpose.

For weeks while the strike lasted, the hotel's managers, took rooms to indulge in catnaps between shifts while logging eighteen-hour days. After about ten days, sleep deprivation and its associated delirium set in. The feeling was one of extreme intoxication, with spatial judgment and cognitive functions impaired. With our brain chemistry altered, we were barely able to engage in rational thought. William saw me one day at the copy machine, and a look of horror came over him. He demanded I go to my sleeping room to get desperately needed rest.

I wondered what human beings would subject themselves to such self-induced physical destruction for a job. The abuse lasted about six weeks. I later realized we didn't do it for the hotel or to keep a job. We did it for one another. Hotel and hospitality workers at the management level train to be deferential. We prepare to please people and to serve our guests. By reasonable extension, we help our fellow associates. We all had a stake in the game, and we needed each other. It was under these circumstances that the bonds of camaraderie were strengthened.

Along the way, our purpose became much more significant than delivering breakfast to a thirtieth-floor suite. Our central mission became helping each other survive another day. Not one of us wanted to be the one to fail. No one wanted to complain we were physically exhausted to the point of diminishing returns. We did it because we knew there was noble satisfaction in seeing this event to its rightful conclusion. We became expert crisis managers moving effortlessly from one raging fire to another. Each success, no matter how small, added a notch to the belt of our professional development. We knew the contingency planning required to survive a massive work stoppage would make us more valuable, versatile, and insightful future leaders.

Co-existing in the hard-boiled, militant union setting was a shocking, if not traumatizing experience for many young managers. Most were trusting, conditioned to walk softly, and unprepared for the adversarial union mentality that was, at times, resistant to the rules of respectful human interaction.

The union environment subsists on a diet of low common denominators. Its existence is bolstered by an unrelenting spirit of workforce homogeneity—dumbing participants down to the middle for the protection of the collective. Therefore, in its purest form, a work stoppage or a union strike is job security by any means necessary.

In his world of limited filtration, William was never at a loss for words when provided an opportunity to rage against the union. He would stand in the middle of a room and, in a fit of hysterical, vein-popping invective, scream bloody murder aimed squarely at the union leadership. After all, it was they who were standing in his way of total control over his environment. A union work stoppage threatened all that was decent, honorable, and good by his standards. The only problem was the union wasn't going away.

For all of William's talent, the obstacle to achieving his goal of sitting in the king's chair at that iconic property was his persona, the complicated part of him. It remained his Achilles heel. Although he still enjoyed the protection of the company's older guard stirring about the corporate office in the rarified air of status emeritus, they were retiring and moving on. Their protection of William was enough to keep him where he was. Still, his personality preceded him. He couldn't convince a newer and more progressive board of directors to elevate him to one of the company's highest-profile positions, and its best compensated.

Tenure and longevity, two most admirable qualities, when misused or taken for granted, are equally disadvantageous. As managers and leaders go about their routines with the customs and practices which have served them well, the march of time changes expectations and sensibilities. Often, long-term leaders rely on familiar methodology and don't feel the gradual shift of sand beneath their feet.

Permanency can be the nemesis of adaptability. As employees age in their workplace, other natural transitions occur. Newer faces begin to populate the environment. They bring different feelings and fresh probabilities. The tenured leader must work to understand changing momentum, to move with it, and make corrective awareness modifications to maintain a sense of relevance. Except William wasn't wired for change.

Today we would say he didn't possess the pedigree. William's antics set him far apart from the contemplative, stately, dignified, politician that was the prototype for the upper echelons of the boardroom. But now in his forties, he felt it was his time. A stranger to measured restraint, his rage intensified each time he was passed over for promotion. Nevertheless, he believed his longevity shielded him, keeping him in his protective bubble. But with his behavior growing more manic, it wasn't long before he became the victim of the outsized opinion he had of himself.

It happened one early evening as two managers sat in his office. It was an opportunity for William to conduct a routine business review. A business discussion with William, perhaps relevant in its original intent, could seamlessly veer off course and transition to a non sequitur observation or denigration of one's style of dress, appearance, weight, or hair color. It didn't matter.

On this occasion, as he gleefully admitted to me later, he leaned in and pointed to the stretched buttonhole on a female manager's shirt, implying she gained weight. Unfortunately, for William, she was not one of his young and terrified, shrinking-violet employees. She was mature, experienced, embarrassed, and outraged. The concept of sexual harassment had recently crept into the workplace lexicon. But for William, the new rules were made for others and not for him.

I recall it took a week to resolve. Staff members were summoned to offer testimonials of their experiences with William. Those who at one time were reluctant to come forward found new voices as their strength grew in numbers. He learned in the most humiliating way that a leader's successes are not only qualified by what he can do for his employer. Nor are they placed in positions of leadership to claim the best prize for themselves. Their work is only complete when they've helped others achieve their goals. For too long, William used his team members as tools, a means to his end. He never learned it wasn't about him.

The company had to take a stand, and after a dozen years, it was over. History, hopes, and aspirations dashed by the misguided point of his finger at a buttonhole. He got away with so much and for so long. Yet, in the face of changing expectations, he couldn't survive his cumulative actions. The workplace universe circled back to its corrective core, and his quirky behavior would no longer be accepted as the tolerable price to pay in exchange for his skillful efficiency.

I chose to take from William what I believed were his better qualities—his business acumen, his ability to move and shift through space, piercing the air with an aura of certainty as he effortlessly planned, directed, and controlled his world while never taking a breath. He told tell me to never stand in the same spot for more than three minutes. He understood it was a business of moving pieces, and most of those pieces would fly by if I stayed in one place too long. The quicker we moved, the more we touched, and the more we learned.

He was twice the age of most of us in his charge, yet we scurried behind him to keep up. If he was running, so should we. It was these qualities I wanted to make my own. And when the opportunity arose, I went with William to his next fiefdom. It was one of the world's largest and most prestigious independently owned restaurants, and so much more. William liked to surround himself with loyal disciples, so it was an arrangement of mutual trust and familiarity, and it was how he slept well at night.

By the usual business metrics, it was the right fit for him. Despite the embarrassing and shameful exit from his previous employer, he landed well. He always told me to aim high, to dot my credentials with impressive brands, and never settle for less than the famous addresses that could open future doors and make people take notice. It was a natural transition for him, and me, to segue from one superstore to another.

It was an iconic destination, set apart from every other dining institution by its famous address, revenue-generating potential, and its undeniable showmanship and style. It was all carefully scripted to be a production full of theatrics, glitz, and glimmer. Whether it was the 500,000 twinkling lights or the gentle snowfall generated from rooftop machinery that blanketed the immense courtyard in winter, it was a show which took on a life of its own, designed to make memories. Its private dining facilities were always in use. It wasn't unusual to host five weddings each weekend out of two rooms, and the enormity of human capital required to facilitate the business's demands was staggering.

It was a cultural shock for William—the free-wheeling Wild West compared to where he and I recently spent the previous years. It was ninety percent bedlam and ten percent profit with an ingrained low-wage culture that teetered on the edge of rebellion. It wasn't the majestic and dignified mini city we loved so much. There weren't benign, corporate uncles, stately politician types, VIPs, or heads of state with whom he used to associate. Patrons came through the doors at a dizzying pace. The lobby was perpetually packed with eager diners just waiting to experience what they heard was more of a magic show than lunch or dinner.

Hotel life seemed much more predictable. We knew in advance who was coming, how many people were arriving, and when they were coming. It was a smooth formula compared to the mega-restaurant behemoth, which always seemed ready to burst at the seams. Because of the volume of people, we struggled with processes, controls, and heightened expectations. In this tumultuous setting, I watched William grapple with his emotional equilibrium.

Cautious and circumspect by nature, I could maintain restraint under almost any circumstance. But William was wired to control his environment and didn't have such a character trait. His manic personality didn't serve him well under extreme conditions. As usual, he raged against those he believed didn't have his sense of urgency and determination. His favorite targets were the managers who controlled the reception desk, the front line of the battle. They were all that stood between the masses of humans, pandemonium, and the inner sanctum of the dining rooms. If they lost control at that strategic point, all hell could break loose with hundreds of hungry guests at the gates.

I was accustomed to seeing William erupt in anger, and usually, it contained a thread of comedic humor. Although his punching bags, the desk managers, were unfamiliar with his volcanic personality. They could never move people fast enough for him, and he stood in their space in blatant ridicule of them, pretending to do their jobs by bellowing out the numbers of those tables ready for new diners. His unsubtle statement was the front desk managers should have had those tables occupied many minutes ago, and they were too slow, or too incompetent, to clear the lobby of the multitudes. Time and again, I saw defeat in their eyes, weary from fighting on two fronts, both the crowd and William.

The problem with being a meddlesome boss is the meddler will get involved just enough not to be helpful. In moments of heightened consciousness, the best action by a boss is sometimes no action because his knee-jerking shifts the staff's focus from managing the mission to handling him. Solving the task becomes more difficult because the insecure boss has added another layer of complexity to an already precarious situation. Unfortunately, William always saw himself as the solution and never the problem.

He regularly socialized with celebrities and pseudo-celebrities, a practice he enjoyed from our hotel days. He was drawn to edgy types, and moving in their orbit fueled the vision of the identity he cautiously assembled for the outside world to see. It was the identity of the well-connected, dominant male, and it was exciting for him to be tangentially connected to their power. To move in those circles only confirmed his rightful place with those who breathed the rarified air of instant recognition, respect, validation, and mystery—the very things he needed to fuel his oversized ego.

One rugged individual, the kind with a small-caliber weapon adorning his ankle, approached William to inquire about staging an event for one hundred fifty of his closest associates. The only problem was William promised him that his attractive catering manager would be delighted to handle all the arrangements. When she realized William's intent, she threatened him with a sexual harassment suit for placing her in a powerless position where she felt objectified.

We form perspective through the grinder of experience and harsh realities. But as William tormented his way through the days, it was evident he hadn't learned a lesson he should have only a couple of years before. Still, there had to be more to his self-sabotaging behavior. He was a man who, by now, reigned over two of the world's most prestigious addresses, which paid him handsomely enough to retire comfortably while still young enough to enjoy the vigor of his relative youth. Yet, he was willing to overlook standards of acceptable behavior to satisfy the demands of his ego.

I often wondered about the inclinations that moved William so close to the perilous place of losing it all. In the final analysis, his mighty ego had too many needs. The ego on fire will not engage the better brain to overrule its darker thoughts and desires. His ego required constant reassurance and stimulation, and he went to great lengths to find it. It was his ego that formed the foundation of his workplace persona. The persona is the mask we wear to signal to the world what we wish to be, and he shaped his cover to meet the needs of his carefully constructed identity. It must have been a terrible burden for him always to wear false bravado.

His persona was one thing, but his demons were another. We possess latent dispositions to variable degrees. They represent the wild, chaotic, and unknown side of ourselves. These shadowy traits form a steady source of creative energy. They add color and texture to our lives. Therefore, character, or how we operate in the world, is a manifestation of the ability to manage those qualities responsibly. It is left to the individual to govern those desires to form a foundation of proper human interaction. Therefore, the person we identify as having a strong character is the one who has learned to sort out such dispositions by separating those that are acceptable from those which should be hidden away.

We are social animals, and cultural interrelation is key to our survival. Our urges and behaviors must align with commonly accepted norms of workplace comportment. It is here where William struggled. He never stood still long enough to do the necessary soul work to connect his emotions with a logical sense of where his actions may lead him. His battle with both his repressed sexuality and determination to demonstrate virile masculinity became the foundation of his instincts, his weaknesses, his desires, and his most embarrassing fears.

I attempted to unravel the mystery of the man who could be kind to me and cruel and uncaring to others. I watched his behavior change from what I initially thought was eccentric overexcitement to a possessed state of agitated and animated fury. Although I came to know him better and manage him more effectively for myself, he became more explosive to others. When triggered, he could transform into a cartoonish version of himself with teeth-clenching, eyes- bulging, vein-popping intensity. For me, he was the ideal psychological study—the archetype model of the fragmented and frenzied mind attempting to organize and structure himself to appear just how he needed. His attempts weren't always successful.

William was a survivor, and he remained in his lofty position for several more years. After, I followed his career as he struggled to find the right fit. We immerse ourselves in a culture. We deploy our routines and rituals to navigate environmental and sociological forces successfully. We create behavioral and operational assumptions based on what gets us through each day. Our associates, accustomed to our quirks and flashpoints, usually provide the benefit of their doubt, until we realize our methodology and habits are ill-suited for a different culture with new sensibilities, customs, and practices.

As a one-dimensional leader, William failed in smaller, more delicate boxes, boutique environments where the spotlight on relationship-building was more intense. He was better suited for the administration of large common denominators, and less equipped for the softer touch of managing individual relationships across generational and organizational lines.

Successfully managing relationships depends on the ability to be vulnerable, to let the other side win now and then, but William was supremely hardwired. Fierce and resolute, he was having none of the evolving management paradigms that should have compelled him to alter his style. Those were always trivial things standing in his way. He couldn't stop being who he was. His methods were inflexibly entwined with his core being, the form making the man.

William showed up unexpectedly for a visit. It was years since I last saw him. Impeccably dressed as always, he looked fit and tanned. I complimented the beautifully tailored, classic salt-and-pepper overcoat he wore that day. He long left the wild world of hotel and restaurant pandemonium and found a comfortable niche in hospital administration. I remember how he looked strangely still, composed, and peaceful. It was in stark contrast to the man I knew who lined his desk drawer with prescription pills.

Perhaps the hospital environment reshaped him. Relentless images of illness and death can change a person. I no longer saw William as the possessed and hysterically agitated character I used to know. Now in his mid-fifties, he survived his rage, and hopefully, he was able to let go of one or two of his little monsters. Most of all, I hoped he finally found peace to survive himself.

Then it happened. About a year later, he was gone at age fifty-five. He tried to keep a part of his life steeped in mystery. I don't know how long he held on to his secret—the deadly illness which eventually took his life and the lives of thousands of other men. For all his demonstrative theatrics, he was still intensely proud. Thoroughly practiced at denial, it was entirely reasonable for him to slip away quietly.

I was saddened and troubled by his untimely passing. I was unsettled because this man of unrelenting and complicated humanity may never have attained what he wanted more than anything. He longed for enduring admiration and acceptance as a respected professional. At least he gained that from me.

I never heard him speak of family, parents, close friends, or a relationship in the period I knew him. He certainly had many acquaintances, yet I sense he was difficult to get close to because he never stopped trying to be someone he wasn't. People gravitate towards others they believe act with authenticity and pure intentions. It's a matter of trust, and he never knew the joy and freedom of being true to himself.

I don't know how to remember a man as unfailingly human as William. He would be in his seventies today, and perhaps time would have softened his edges. If I had the opportunity, I would like to have shown him the column list at the top of this chapter. I would ask him to check off all the words he believes described him in his younger days. With his distinguished economy of movement, I think he would have taken a red marker and slashed a thick line through all of it with his own words, "All the above."

Chapter 4

SAM, THE GOOD CHEF

"I always say that I don't believe I'm a chef. I try to be a storyteller." — *Jose Andres*

SAM WAS A mountain of a man in more ways than one. He was an extraordinarily gifted chef, easy-going, and with natural confidence. He could turn chopped meat into filet mignon, and that was before he put much effort into it. He was charmingly immature, a big kid at heart, a clown, a friend, and a deeply troubled man who was as difficult to manage as he was easy to forgive.

He had immense girth and a larger-than-life personality—a five-hundred-pound man who could go to a strip club and have all the pretty dancers hanging on his every word. The French call this gravitas—we called him the Good Chef. He was accommodating and generous to a fault, and to know him was to love him.

He was the Good Chef because he could light up a room and disarm anyone who had the mere thought of a bad intention. He didn't move fast because he didn't have to. Strong as an ox, he was the gentlest of giants. His voice barely raised above a soft monotone because he never had to yell to call attention to himself. He was a man of natural charm, the compellingly attractive kind that inspired devotion from others.

Sam had a profound sense of duty and loyalty, so he was easy to count on. He would never knowingly displease anyone, especially me, whom he considered a friend and mentor. But this time, I needed him—desperately.

I set out to rebrand one of our restaurants from an expensive, southern grille to a friendlier Italian concept. The menu change was initially on Chef Jim. It doesn't sound like a difficult task because people cook at home. The home cook can do as they please. Precision and timing are less crucial when there aren't one hundred fifty hungry paying customers looking at the chef's back. But in the highly charged, professional environment, it is a painstaking process. It is a difficult undertaking of carefully planned action steps taking at least a week or more of preparation before serving a morsel to a customer. The longer the menu, the longer the process.

When chefs make menu changes, you can count on a bustle of activity in their kitchen leading to the implementation date. They are testing, tasting, slicing, and dicing new food items for hours at a time. They are buying plates and accessories to make their new dishes look better. However, this was different because I didn't see the usual buzz in Jim's kitchen, even though he reassured me he was on schedule. I kept asking for an initial draft of a menu that never came. By Friday, just three days before zero hour, it was apparent he had failed. All along, I suspended my disbelief that he might do the unthinkable—which was nothing. I could deal with him later, but for now I needed a new plan. I just didn't have anywhere to start, until I thought of Sam, the Good Chef.

I went to him with my hat in my hands. Knowing he took the weekend off, I begged him to save me, and us, from total embarrassment. He said, "OK. Get a piece of paper." Almost reflexively, he rattled off a menu of about fifteen items. He said, "Go type it up. That's our menu." He arrived the next day at noon, holding a bunch of grocery bags from the supermarket. He couldn't get a delivery from our primary supplier on such short notice, so he went to the store and shopped for a menu of items he would prepare.

In the meantime, there was a large pot of simmering red sauce on the stove in another kitchen. Every Italian restaurant has its "Sunday sauce." It is the foundation for a substantial portion of the menu. Sam asked me to go to the other kitchen and check on the sauce since he knew I grew up with Italian cooking, and I could tell by the aroma if it had enough oregano and garlic. I walked into the kitchen, sniffed around, and my spirits rose. When he got around to making that perfect sauce was anyone's guess. Maybe at five o'clock in the morning.

Sam was in complete command with a small army of cooks around him. All of them moved purposefully with invisible eyes on the clock. No one said a word because they hung on his words. I stayed back to remain out of everyone's way. He barked out orders, never having to raise his voice. His presence and his demeanor spoke for him. I still had the paper he dictated to me the night before. He made changes, added new ingredients, and altered preparations along the way. Sometimes, he changed the whole dish. He sensed my anxiety about losing time. He just smiled and said, "Don't you worry. Now try this," as he kept feeding me small samples of something he just created. He effortlessly made it up as he went along. Something about a wing and a prayer came to mind, and he hardly broke a sweat.

Sam spent Saturday creating fifteen new spectacular recipes from supermarket ingredients. Later that night, he had to record everything for the recipe book, so the following day, the other cooks could do just what he did, like reading from a script. That is the tricky part—getting inside the other cooks' heads, so, like a symphony, the mechanics and timing are precise. He obtained an emergency food delivery for Sunday, so he didn't have to go back to the supermarket. Seeing the eighteen-wheel truck, I breathed a sigh of relief. Sam worked all day

Sunday practicing the new dishes until they were perfect. By the evening, we were exhausted but ready for Monday.

The Good Chef did what I thought was unachievable. I remember that weekend as he kept smiling, he told me doing the impossible wasn't too difficult. It just took him a little while longer.

Sam was the perfect candidate for gastric bypass surgery. He was destined for an early grave if he didn't have the procedure. He wasn't well in the aftermath of the operation. Part of his intestines choked off during the process, resulting in septic shock. He was rushed to emergency surgery and lapsed into a coma. He awoke about a week later after coming close to death. When I asked Sam what a near-death experience was like, he said he was in a painless, dreamlike place where fairies danced in his head. That would certainly qualify as a painless place. But little did anyone know the hurt he endured.

Before the operation, Sam lost his childhood friend, his best friend, in a tragic one-car accident. In his profound grief, he smiled through it. He never shed a tear or asked for a day off. I found his demeanor to be uncommonly stoic for a man who just lost his oldest and dearest friend under horrific circumstances. His reaction, or lack thereof, was either the bearing of a man expert at putting life's happenstances in boxes, or perhaps, similarly practiced at unhealthy denial. Nevertheless, it was a foreshadowing of things to come.

There was something else about the Good Chef, a pulse I couldn't put my finger on. Some people are easily sized up, their book always open, but I had a sneaking suspicion there was more to the man than the easy-going seductive charm and larger-than-life bearing. Cautious by nature, I always gave Sam only about eighty percent of my trust bank. Knowing people can be an unexpected source of disappointment, I placed the other twenty percent in my emotional reserve account.

It is easy to say we should love and trust as if never hurt, except human nature is smarter than people think. If left alone, it will send appropriate warning signals. It wasn't that his persona wasn't genuine. It was that he perfected it effortlessly. I further sensed that the man's outward manifestations were at least, in part, a mask presented to satisfy the demands of his environment and not representative of the full inner personality.

Following his surgery, the Good Chef, like others who have encountered a near-death experience, seemed to arrive at a new awareness of his life's meaning and purpose. Raymond Moody first codified these experiences in his 1975 book *Life After Life*. He proposed that near-death survivors feel a renewed sense of self-esteem with a measurable change in attitude marked by a re-examination of existing relationships.[i] Therefore, it is common, for example, that divorce rates are high among those in this group.

Dr. Steven Taylor in *Out of the Darkness, From Turmoil To Transformation* refers to the aftermath of brushes with mortality as a period of "flourishing."[ii] He writes that intense encounters of our demise increase our ability to be more mindful of the present and more vividly aware of our surroundings. Taylor further describes the sensation as a re-orienting of attention away from the past, and the future, with a passionate desire to make up for lost opportunity by intensely focusing on the here and now. So perhaps not coincidentally, the Good Chef embraced life like never before.

However, something else was happening. About two hundred fifty pounds lighter, Sam reveled in all he missed while tipping the scales at five hundred. In his awakening, he became a man on a mission, singular in purpose, but reckless in its application. The surgery may have relieved a symptom, but it didn't address the cause. The eating addiction and the heedlessness that marked his march to morbid obesity changed its face.

There is a documented connection between gastric bypass and alcoholism. According to the Ria Health Institute, bariatric surgery alters the body's hormones. These hormones influence how hungry we get, and the reward we get from eating, but they can also influence alcohol consumption. Drinking more after surgery may be a complicated result of greater reward and altered body chemistry.[iii] It turns out that twenty percent of people who have had gastric bypass surgery develop an alcohol use disorder. That is more than three times the rate of the general population.

Sam's stomach, now one-third the size, couldn't hold what it was used to, although liquids could go right through. It began innocently enough with an occasional cocktail after work, a hospitality worker's tradition. Then the alcohol made its way into the workplace, and I noticed behavioral changes. He arrived at the office later, leave earlier, and I heard rumors he was hitting bars and wrecking cars.

He fell in love with a pretty lady. He pined for her going back to the days when he knew his immense size was an inhibitor to winning at love. As appealing as his personality was, it was no match for his less attractive, massive physical frame. But now that he was adequately proportioned, he had the great equalizer, a new formula for success. At least in his mind, the package was complete. She would undoubtedly fall in love with him this time. She had to.

The chase became Sam's defining work. With his obsessive personality in overdrive, he would make her fall in love with him. His full-on pursuit of her was almost childlike. She was the object, the trophy, the vision of intimacy, and validation he desperately wanted. She came to visit me knowing how close I was to him. She asked me what I thought she should do with the Good Chef. She wanted my affirmation that he was right for her before she gave him her heart.

She liked him, but she didn't love him. I didn't resent her desire for a few sensory pleasures, even though she didn't detect his vulnerability. I asked her to let him go and allow him to live his life. She was enjoying his attention, his undying affection, and his pleasant company. Sam was the clingy type, so he wasn't going away if he believed he still had a chance.

Perhaps she wasn't using him in its most manipulative context, yet she was undoubtedly enjoying his pursuit of her. At the same time, I was growing perturbed with the Good Chef. He was a grown man who made his adult choices. As stubborn as he was in his quest for affection, his heightened desire for intimacy didn't allow him to see that she was in it for the wrong reasons. Even his near-death experience wasn't enough to earn him the things he wanted most—love, intimacy, and affection.

She eventually left the company and the relationship. A short while later, she became engaged. She held the wedding reception where Sam still worked, where we all worked, our band of friends. I know Sam was embarrassed, crushed. But as usual, his outward expression belied his hurt and his sorrow.

I remember the worst part of the day was when he had to cook—for her wedding. It was insult leveled after injury. He wasn't a crier. Instead, he continued to seek comfort inside of a cheap bottle. I wouldn't have been surprised if he drank his way through the wedding. I believe I purposely stayed away from his kitchen that day, fearful I might find him in a state of complete disrepair. If he had only one thing left, it was his professional pride and unrelenting sense of duty. Like a good soldier donning his uniform, Sam put on his whites, and he cooked—for her.

I invited my senior leadership team to a Christmas gathering at a nice restaurant. I was already seated and waiting for my guests, where I could see the door. Sam strolled in, and I knew it immediately. We were gathered in the spirit of celebration, and he couldn't keep his head out of his plate as he stuttered, stammered, and bumbled his way through the evening. We were all stunned, angered, and saddened by his audacity and that he couldn't stay sober for one evening with his closest associates. I wanted to ask him to leave, but he arrived with someone else, and I feared he wouldn't get home in one piece if left alone.

By now, he was too damaged, in free fall to a dark, depressive place. Shortly after that, I had to terminate his employment when he stumbled into work one morning; his once commanding voice reduced to incoherent drivel. It was one of the hardest things I ever had to do. However, I quickly righted myself knowing I did all I could for him with repeated warnings it would come to this. Many people recognized his slow descent into addiction. He later bounced around from job to job and from one relationship to another. He seemed to be reaching but never grasping, looking, and never finding.

Addicts lie, and at one point, Sam convinced me he had found sobriety. I worked on a business plan and wanted a chef-partner. I invited him to meet me at a potential location. In his perpetual denial, he arrived reeking of alcohol. I decided there was nothing more I could give him, and I walked away.

He was an excellent liar because his charisma preceded him, and he could convince the hardest skeptic, and himself, that he was clean and sober. And that is the thing about charisma. It only exists in the context of a relationship. No one has it when they are sitting alone in a darkened room. As his relationships fractured, so did the larger-than-life magnetism, replaced with despair and the blurred imaginings of once-great things.

As Sam spiraled deeper, it became almost impossible to connect with him. I lost track of him through all the lies, the job losses, the arrests, the unhealthy relationships, and the misadventures. He was like a ghost, popping in and out of lives. It was his way of convincing the world that he was a man on the move, a busy man, a whole man with a full life to live.

As he hung by a thread on a small-town reputation of fading greatness, there was always someone ready and willing to give him another chance. I met some of them. All they could do was shake their heads when his name came up, knowing they banked their reputation, their business, and their trust in someone who sold them a damaged bill of goods. His last job was at a prestigious country club. After a few months, Sam's demons reappeared, and he stopped showing up for work. They later found him wandering the Philippines.

He came home, and he drank. Girlfriends hid his bottles. Alcoholics think of ingenious ways to consume their vice of choice. Ray Milland's Don Birnam character in *The Lost Weekend* comes to mind. Birnam hid his bottles high up in ceiling lamps to avoid detection by family members. Others put it in their salad dressing. Sometimes they feign illness so they can consume copious amounts of Nyquil or sip from a water bottle containing vodka.

In the early morning hours of March 2nd, 2017, they found him, motionless, curled up in the back seat of his Jeep. His girlfriend had expelled him from their residence when he arrived reeking of cheap wine. On that night, the Good Chef went to Walmart. He was most likely shopping for a short stay at a local hotel until such time when he could, hopefully, be welcomed back in his home. After two days without a word from him, he was reported missing. They tracked his cell phone to the location of the parking lot where his mother found him. He was forty-three, deceased from years of drug and alcohol abuse that irreparably damaged his heart. As Sam took his final breaths, his last visions of life on earth were the dispassionate faces of passing strangers. And that is how addicts die—alone.

We, those in our tight little group, went to his memorial service. Uncharacteristic for a funeral, every eye in the chapel was dry. The mood felt unsurprisingly light and relaxed. The Good Chef never cried, and no one cried on this day either. Human nature is funny that way. It tells us when our minds can be free of regret, unbound by self-recrimination. Life is for the living, and we spent our collective compassion long ago chasing the ghost of the man we affectionately used to know as the Good Chef.

It was as if we all knew the elephant in the room. For months we had ringside seats to a tragedy playing out in slow motion. On that day, there was nothing more to give. While there, I curiously looked for the girl he almost died for. The one that got away. And in a way, he did die for her. Maybe now she would show, although I didn't see her. I thought to myself, perhaps at least metaphorically, that she managed to get away from him in life and now in his death.

And there it was—the polished brass urn of ashes with an oversized photo of Sam beside it. That was all that remained of him. They say that God only gives us what we can handle. I just wish he hadn't put so much trust in the Good Chef.

Chapter 5

MICHAEL AND THE
STEALTH WARRIOR

*"Our careers, and our lives, can be shaped by few people—
especially the ones we don't see coming."* — *Unknown*

WHAT IS THE tolerable price to pay for gainful employment? For
Michael, it was a deal with the devil, a profoundly perplexing experience of external conflict and internal struggle. It was a relentless assault
on his value system that kept him awake, wondering how to navigate
the next day's minefield of interrogations, preposterous insinuations,
condemnations, and the stupefying indictments of his character and
integrity. Astonishingly, one person, a single roguish mind was capable
of engineering all of it.

Until then, Machiavelli was only a name, a term Michael knew
from history books. But his life was imitating 17th-century literature,
with its pretense of virtue, wide-ranging deception, tragic waste, re-
venge, anger, and manipulation of reasoning—the kind that turns foul
into fair. Michael's story, like a Shakespearean paradox, reflects the

irony of life, a sudden reversal of fortune, where calamity and suffering contrast with previous happiness and success.

Michael was an admired and respected leader. He spent years building and leading successful teams under the most difficult circumstances. With the mental DNA of a diagnostic mechanic, he intuitively recognized deficiencies. A bold thinker, he enjoyed the challenge of deconstructing failed templates of operations and then recreating them—a quality that came naturally to him. With the building blocks of a successful career already assembled, he hoped his reputation would reflect his many accomplishments, and they did—until he met a stealth warrior.

Michael obtained his position as a result of the stealth warrior's promotion, who was Michael's new boss. However, it quickly became evident that the stealth one's elevation was based on a very narrow aptitude and made possible by absent and detached overseers. He left Michael with a broken and unhealthy culture of performance mediocrity and uncivil behavior. The team operated without professional boundaries for so long that they internalized and normalized the abuse they were freely permitted to engage in under the stealth one's negligent supervision.

It takes a daring leader with an active intellect to turn thoughts into actions. However, the mentally lazy stealth warrior functioned under the illusion that any corrective action would cause team resentment—a counterintuitive, head-scratching, non-strategy that defied logic and defined his passivity. He only interceded to repair shortcomings, operational or behavioral, when they affected his comfort and security.

The goal of a weak leader is to provide for their safety first. The difficult decisions they make advance their agenda exclusively. They place themselves and their interests ahead of their team members because they cannot register the attributes that define courageous and decisive leadership. Fundamental insecurity shapes their inaction to challenging situations because confronting deficiencies is messy. The strong leader examines outcomes in advance to win, while the feckless boss only evaluates consequences to avoid the anxiety of losing.

The assured and confident leader knows to detach when they leave their legacy in the hands of a new guardian. It should have been a natural transition of stewardship from the stealth one to Michael. Unfortunately, it wasn't in the stealth warrior's ego composition to separate from his previous relationships, and he formed emotional attachments to those he hired years before. He went to great lengths to protect them from any offense short of, perhaps, attempted murder. He designed and encouraged systems to enrich them unduly, and he looked the other way at the chaos wrought by his lack of generalship.

It was a sad testimonial to the environment barbarians routinely create—the classic cocktail of toxicity characterized by not hiring professionally minded team members resulting in malignant behavior, then, ignoring the wreckage. The tentative, and ineffectual leader sometimes won't recognize noxious behavior or its effect on others. Fearful of bold action, and not made for stress, they tap dance around prickly issues because of an inability to confront others constructively. Unfortunately, the stealth warrior wouldn't allow Michael to correct it.

Waging battles on two fronts left Michael with little room to pivot. He was caught between staff members who were never managed, permitted to scorch the earth, and each other—and a newly promoted boss mainly concerned with preserving the ruinous remnants of his previous handiwork. So for Michael to be effective, he had to have corrective and challenging conversations with individuals accustomed to operating with special protections made possible by his predecessor.

There is a thin line between quiet confidence and conceit. The calm, worldly perspective that comes from enduring life's realities cannot peacefully coexist with immaturity, insecurity, and hubris. It was in this alternate existence where Michael's skills of patience and diplomacy challenged him to his limits. The hard part was remaining successful without losing his identity or relinquishing his expectations.

Michael had full responsibility, yet only half of the authority due to the stealth one's meddlesome ways. Michael anticipated that the stealth one would at least have a passing acquaintance with self-awareness, perhaps just enough to step outside of himself and disengage from what was no longer in his immediate charge. But Michael was wrong. In his decades of leadership, he never had to fight a boss with just enough knowledge to be dangerous—one thoroughly determined to preserve his legacy of systemic failure, and his inflamed ego. And be aware of the sincerely ignorant anti-leader with just enough information.

Dr. Gleb Tsipursky, the author of *The Truth Seeker's Handbook*, describes the overconfident manager who is blindly optimistic about their limited expertise. Unable to recognize defects or the gaps in their knowledge, they use their authority status to shape and control an illusory bias and manipulate reasoning. Consequently, the world seems in alignment with the narrow view they force-feed onto those less aware.[iv]

One of a barbarian's indispensable weapons is information management. It is a necessary ingredient in a noxious brew of hegemony to influence and control a false narrative—one they earnestly believe. But for the barbarian to legitimize the tales they tell themselves about those they despise, they must obtain validation from other less informed allies—supporters whose sole source of information is the barbarian.

Once it was apparent that Michael had the knowledge, and self-confidence to challenge the stealth one's dominion, he made Michael the target of his ire by setting up an information pipeline for Michael's employees. Any disagreement with an employee, however inconsequential, was expanded beyond reasonable proportions, especially if it involved one of the warrior's previous hires—the ones he sought to protect. When Michael felt the need to take such matters to human resources, the barbarian threatened to make the employee's complaints public. It was an appalling level of emotional blackmail and back-door wickedness Michael had never experienced from another human being. Nevertheless, the stealth one, free to revel in his self-importance, was managing other senior leaders and in charge of an entire division of the company.

As if playing a cynical game of "gotcha," the stealth one seized upon every chance to express authority by turning simple misunderstandings into fatal errors. He magnified each perceived or real offense more than deserved, and he rarely let an opportunity pass where he wasn't reminding Michael of an alleged shortcoming.

It wasn't unusual for the stealth one to accuse Michael of mismanaging a routine disagreement among coworkers, even though the incident occurred two levels down in the organization's hierarchy—on his day off. He blamed Michael for orchestrating the demise of a manager, one of the stealth one's previous hires, which would have resulted in complete operational turmoil. It didn't matter to the stealth warrior that the manager's termination for cause was due to a third-party contract violation, costing the company thousands of dollars.

The barbarian designed his criticisms with deliberation. He delivered them with injurious intent without a pretense of lucidity or a fundamental consideration of the reality of situations. But as often as Michael attempted to steel his resolve to remain professional and calm in the face of inhumane and unfair treatment, he still felt diminished. Unfortunately, Michael recognized early in his tenure that his management challenge was this new and strange breed of barbarian—a devil in disguise thoroughly practiced in organizational skullduggery.

Stealth warrior-barbarians are covert narcissists who act clandestinely, although they don't necessarily spring from a dark place. Unlike the explosive, anti-leaders who communicate with excitable condescension, stealth warriors speak softly and deliberately. They appear almost shy and humble and easily mingle with coworkers. Their relaxed and even-tempered persona is captivating and reassuring. They help, smile, and sympathize, and conduct themselves respectfully while surreptitiously worming their way into unsuspecting minds. Their easygoing nature is a cover used to offer up incoherent conclusions as facts. And like a magician, they are practiced at presenting not how conditions are, but how they can make them appear to be.

Inexperienced with meaningful confrontation, the stealth one usually attacked from the blindside, rendering Michael disarmed and unprepared for an assault on his good sense, or judgement. Think of a major league baseball pitcher with a carefully slow release. The pitcher's effectiveness is primarily rooted in the deceptiveness of his delivery of the ball to home plate. His pitching motion is deliberate and methodical, lulling the batter's sensory receptors, but only until the ball explodes out of the pitcher's hand with blazing velocity that reaches the batter in less than one half of one second. The hitter's brain must furiously process what his eyes have seen, usually with failure as a result.

Like the batter whose mind tries to play catch-up, Michael had to work feverishly to make practical sense of the stealth one's severed logic. To Michael's profound bewilderment, the warrior faulted him for chasing away a potential senior job candidate—during the interview process! The candidate never worked for the company and made a family decision not to relocate from his hometown for a lateral career move. It was a preposterous, jaw-dropping accusation, and like others, they were seismic shocks to Michael's sensibilities. When the attacks came, Michael didn't have time to unravel the mangled entrails of barbarian reasoning and assemble a compelling response. His reaction to such assaults was naturally defensive, to which he was criticized for being, well, defensive. But he knew he had to react to save his credibility, or his livelihood, or both.

For Michael, it became a full-time job to successfully predict how his boss, with his numerous triggers, would respond to regular exchanges of information. Indeed, routine discussions about office personnel could, without warning, degenerate into a personal attack based entirely on a false supposition, with the warrior's meandering notions advanced as facts. It forced Michael into an anxious position of proving *what didn't happen* and fight for his innocence, which devalued his authority as a responsible leader. It was as if the stealth one moved in an otherworldly existence of orphaned ideas that were uniquely his, seeing the world through a dense fog, and detached from the reality of commonly accepted standards and norms.

Michael was like a Shakespearean character in the throes of inner turmoil. Eventually, he became exhausted from engaging the ghosts residing in the warrior's mind—a mind fixated on Michael's destruction. No employee can survive in an environment shaped by an individual with evil intent, who is shameless of shameful behavior, and whose thinking can't be altered by reason.

Nevertheless, Michael was raised to stand his ground in the face of tyranny, and he chose respectful confrontation. He also knew he was pushing a boundary with someone comfortable engaging in unethical, and possibly immoral activities. Unfortunately, the preservation of one's authenticity and dignity usually comes with a hefty price, and Michael was dying inside, drained by the constant fight to preserve his pride. What should have been a celebration of his many successes became a pitched battle for his psychological safety. The creative energy he should have spent maximizing productivity and opportunity for his company shifted to a primal defense of all he knew to be reasonable and right.

In all his years, Michael's bosses wanted what was best for his personal and professional development. Even on occasions of disagreement, he always knew where he stood because both he and his superior sought the same result—to advance the company's mission and vision. Leadership is a partnership, and responsible bosses laid tracks for him to follow while removing obstacles in his path. Yet the stealth one *was* the obstacle, holding Michael accountable to impossible ideals that were unattainable by any rational grasp of human nature. Unfortunately, this baffling anti-leader was intent on weaponizing nature against him. In all his years of leadership, Michael never knew another human being willing to confiscate his esteem, self-worth and his livelihood so effortlessly.

That is where the management of the ego is most effective. Ego management is an equalizer. It levels the playing surface because it standardizes and highlights team goals while clearing the field for individual participants' needs to be right. When everyone's requirements are in remission, philosophical differences are complementary offsets, not a battle for intellectual supremacy.

It could have been an agonizing, slow death of Michael's confidence if not for the unshakeable certainty of his accomplishments, and awareness of his value as a leader. With the benefit of events in rearview, I asked Michael what he could have done differently to minimize the angst of his experience. His brow creased, and his lips pursed while he scrolled his brain for an alternate strategy he could have deployed which might have led to a more positive outcome. He concluded quite philosophically that not every relationship is fated to be successful. People grow and develop in different chapters in time. The most productive relationships are those where collective beliefs and goals are in alignment simultaneously. When misalignment occurs, conflict is an inevitable result.

We aren't made for everyone, and we don't have the option to select who evaluates us. Barbarians may openly and brazenly criticize us because they haven't learned where their emotions are taking them. People will disappoint us. That is human nature. As we progress in our careers, we have many ebbs and flows, high points, and low points. One bad experience doesn't define us. When we've worked long enough, the margins to be someone's lousy story expands, fairly or unfairly. The benefit of doubt isn't promised to anyone.

The illustration of the stealth warrior is not unique. Across the business landscape, we promote good employees and middle managers who are perhaps highly skilled in a specific capacity or subject matter. The result is a generation of managers with a wealth of industry knowledge but inadequate leadership competency because we failed to provide necessary people training. In the haste to fill a void in the administration of company business, we elevate peak performers without assessing their fitness to deploy softer skills, such as effective confrontation, conflict resolution, listening, and processing feedback. Although desirable, the skills that made the manager effective in their defined function—organization, control, and planning, aren't prerequisites to the successful leadership of men and women with a wide latitude of needs.

We define evil as the absence of goodness. But we can choose to see goodness. The ability to make conscious decisions is what separates human beings from all other creatures. It was not an accident of fate that the creator changed the mold for one group. One species had to be imbued with the faculty of the mind to advance humanity and create order in the world. From a metaphysical viewpoint, the desire to enrich, lift, and inspire is the natural law of being. Conversely, it is unnatural that we are on this earth for any other reason. It is the only explanation for why some people gravitate towards responsible leadership that elevates, connects, and nurtures minds.

That is why it is essential to know our barbarians. They are the anti-models, the constant reminders that we have the gift of choice. We can choose common decency.

Chapter 6

$$\sim\!\!\sim\!\!\sim$$

FRED THE EVIL GENIUS,
BUT WITH A SMALL "E"

"The essence of genius is to know what to overlook."
— *William James*

BY THE LATE '80s, the city's downtown was home to only two super luxury hotels. That seemed to be enough until a new hotel was born, positioned as an independent boutique, and built within the confines of a luxury office building complex. It was on the edge of the financial district, which was a no man's land after five p.m. It sat beneath another psychological barrier, the ugly elevated highway behemoth that cut a menacing swath through the center of the city.

It would take a visionary leader to create a new brand without the history, the pedigree, or the national marketing profile of the two already proven luxury giants. It was against this business landscape that the opportunity made the man, and there was a man tailor-made for the job. We'll call him Fred.

With many years to reflect, my understanding of this leader has evolved. I now see a dynamic, charming, and innovative man through the more transparent lens of a belated professional epiphany. Therefore, he is my evil genius, but with a small "e." There were indeed occasions when he tiptoed the line of barbarity. However, perspectives lie in the realm of the subjective, processed through the mill of personal experience. They belong exclusively to the individual. It is only with time that we synthesize emotions and perceptions to develop a broader appreciation of people and events.

Fred was a man who thoroughly and exceptionally leveraged the authoritative leadership style. It was described later by the groundbreaking social psychologist, Daniel Goleman, as the most effective leadership technique. Fred's manner, as Goleman outlines, is the one that most closely resembles the conventional idea of leadership. His was the classic type often depicted in literature and the media as an inspiring, positive force.[v] He was supremely self-confident with an uncanny ability to know his customer. With the ability to move his team by the strength of his personality, he clearly understood the big prize.

With an infectious sense of energy and enthusiasm, he was always a step ahead of everyone else. Like a wind-up toy, he spoke faster, processed information more quickly, moved more swiftly, and challenged his underlings to keep up with him. His every move and each step spoke to his commitment to achieving results that were only attainable with unrelenting passion, purpose, and perseverance.

Fred was a student of the European schools of hospitality. In that rigorous apprenticeship model, underlings learn by imitation from a stern maestro, and Fred studied well. A mathematician in a former life, he mostly saw the workplace through a series of precise transactions. He strove for perfection in a setting of many moving pieces, and he had difficulty settling for mere excellence.

He was demanding, direct, opinionated, precise, and brilliant. At times he barely masked his impatience with those he believed didn't take complete ownership of their roles as he did. Nevertheless, he could flash signs of empathy. He was a gifted and natural storyteller, and his charismatic and self-deprecating sense of humor spared him from narrowly missing an opportunity to be a total barbarian.

He certainly had the temperament, the predisposition, the tightly wrapped persona, and the overwhelming desire for unquestioned control over his domain to be a magnificent barbarian. However, he also possessed a quality lacking in most of them—the innate capacity to feel. I always sensed there was underlying humanity just waiting to emerge from his nervous intensity.

When I met Fred, I was a stranger in a strange town. Previously, I made stops at iconic locations, including perhaps the most famous hotel name in the world and one of the nation's largest, if not the most successful, restaurant brands. They were sizeable militant, union environments. Until then, success was measured by managing through adversity and the ability to move to where the action was.

Battle-hardened victories came from an uncanny ability to be in the right place at the right time, to move fast, to plan and control, and to establish critical oversight when necessary. Those talents, the ones that served me well in the past, were admirable, although inadequate when running a small, European-style boutique hotel. This new situation required different skills. It was a matter of reverse scalability. In most circumstances, we are asked to ramp up and to intensify energy levels to meet new demands. In the boutique model, we counter-balance, or temper momentum to master the emotional nimbleness needed for a more intimate setting.

However, I was no longer in the union environment where I donned a suit of armor every day. I would have to adapt and adjust my abilities to a new and stately environment. In an abrupt turnabout, I learned that I was to be evaluated almost exclusively on qualitative successes. For Fred, the style was just as important as substance. How we ran the race was as equally significant as the result. It was a matter of how we presented our product to a discerning public. Every move was a tactical component of a more robust marketing strategy.

I had never met a man like Fred. Managing his personality required new muscles to flex, like deftness and finesse. He was a specialist at defining processes, and there was never a flight available by the seat of one's pants. He was a model of dignity in a demanding existence that required precision and a sizeable investment in time, almost to the point where human cloning was the only effective relief.

I struggled with his intense desire for perfection. He had his obsessions that were oddly out of step with broader realities. Sometimes ninety percent compliance is good enough because quality and time are opposing values. His decree that each sugar bowl consist of six white packets, two blue and two pinks each time presented, was perplexing. Fred visited the bustling outdoor summer café daily, and in his double-breasted, navy blue suit, he'd bend down to examine the offending sugar containers to count their contents. It was his way of inspecting what he expected.

If this mandate seemed impractical, my attempt to explain its importance to a group of hospitality students, recruited from colleges for the summer, was equally glib. Fortunately, as wide-eyed, fresh-faced, and-eager-to-please future managers, benign neglect was a concept they hadn't learned yet, and most did their best to follow along. More often than not, I filled the bowls out of Fred's line of sight to shield my neophyte staff and myself—from Fred.

He had a fixation on waste, and alcohol was the object of his preoccupation. His certainty that liquor was a boundless source of irresponsibility was so strong that he asked me to gather the previous evening's empty bottles. After draining the dregs from four dozen bottles, I recovered less than an ounce that I presented to Fred in a measuring cup. His eyes blazed with eager excitement as he exclaimed, "You see? They are wasting liquor!" I remember the feeling of utter worthlessness that it took an hour from my day only to confirm his worst suspicions about an insignificant amount of liquor.

Nevertheless, I was learning to manage him, and I resisted the urge to challenge his unwavering belief that my bartenders were mishandling the hotel's assets. Discretion before valor, I remained silent. I could defend my employees' honor, and mine or I could walk away with a little less of my soul, hoping the incident would fade away. It was safer to let him believe my employees were neglectful and that I had little control over their indiscretions, rather than openly disagree with him. It was classic entrapment that left me reeling, searching for a safe place to land.

He was a machine of meticulousness with specific designs and solutions, gathered over decades of personal experience. He could forcefully communicate the result he wanted, although he didn't take the time to teach the playbook. His authoritativeness was effective when establishing goals, but it was less valuable when creating general feelings of positivity by providing a clear direction.

In fairness, Fred couldn't divine the limitations of our knowledge. He expected that his executive staff create the necessary windows of opportunity to sell their needs, and have the forethought to ask him for guidance. However, this was an exercise in telepathy, if not futility, because of his hectic schedule. We found his door closed for extended periods. Business happens in real-time, and Fred was substantially inaccessible for a man who insisted on communication to the point of micro-management.

With Fred's pronounced desire for control, some staff members were guilty by the flash of his temper until proven innocent. He based his intractable opinions and evaluations on very few encounters, and once he decided someone was a misaligned piece of his puzzle, he made sure they knew their place in his world.

Among Fred's many talents was his ability to know his audience. He designed successful marketing programs that set our hotel apart from the others. Unfortunately, this placed the Marketing Director in Fred's line of fire. Perhaps his worst indiscretion was he didn't provide plans and solutions fast enough, leaving Fred to wonder why he needed a marketing director when he could perform the job himself. They jousted almost daily, and it left the rest of us relieved that Fred's ire was directed elsewhere, at least for the time being.

The storeroom manager, someone who presided over the safe-keeping of hundreds of products, was often and openly maligned as an irresponsible and lethargic steward of the hotel's assets. His sin was maybe, a few misplaced wine boxes sitting on the floor. Unfortunately, Fred never missed an opportunity to diminish the manager's standing among his peers.

I was running out of ways to protect my staff from Fred's meandering condemnations of their performance. If I supported my employees, I was validating their shortcomings, and indirectly, my own. However, if I allowed Fred to believe his criticism was accurate, I also had to admit my failure to direct and control my team members. For a young leader, negotiating Fred's maze of emotional landmines was a nerve-wracking experience that weakened my optimism and diminished my resolve.

I have yet to see an employee thrive under harassing conditions or the threat of termination. In most cases, the authority figure already has the ultimate power to control the failing employee's status. That is all that is needed to implement the resolution they most likely seek. I want to believe when these situations occur, the boss is clumsily attempting to be corrective, but emotions get in the way.

By today's standards, Fred would be considered the remnant of a bygone era. Contemporary management sensibilities teach us that leaders know it is in the organization's best interest to occasionally take the staff's temperature and recognize opportunities for an adjustment in tactics. But Fred was not inclined to check in on himself to reassess his position or his thinking.

Over the years, I have thought about my past relationship with him. We are inclined to believe the best of people, and we suspend our disbelief at their worst. Fred was generous, noble, charitable, and capable of forgiveness. Despite his legendary impatience, he forgave me and others quite often. However, since he was a man always on the move, he could never find the time to provide what most of his team wanted from him. And that was his vast knowledge.

Wisdom is difficult to grasp and internalize when taught in fleeting sound bites. Skillful teachers communicate the method that leads to change. They deliver information with deliberation and purpose. They feel immense personal satisfaction and measure their success by knowing they were a contributing influence on their pupils' future accomplishments. But since Fred was conditioned to manage the collective, the common denominators, he was rarely available to manage or to teach the individual.

I believe Fred fancied himself a great teacher. In some respects, he was. However, he wasn't built to be a naturally effusive instructor free with his advice. He never stayed in one place long enough to develop future leaders, and giving freely of himself wasn't in his DNA. He expected we should watch, learn, and ask questions later.

It is only now with a view through the arc of time that I have a greater appreciation for this imaginative leader. Like most successful leaders, he was a contradiction. The Rutgers School of Business describes leadership as situational. A style that might work under some circumstances might not work in others.[vi] In other words, management needs to be adapted to fit a specific mission, and I believe Fred's method was a key ingredient to his and our success. Had he used a different approach, he might not have achieved the same results.

He possessed at least three qualities great leaders have: a clear vision and direction, a passion for the company and its people, and an ability to inspire trust. No matter what we thought of Fred's demanding ways, we always believed he had the right answer. I eventually realized it was a sense of trust that defined his leadership. He not only had a vision, but he also made sure everyone bought into it. We had faith in him because he displayed his knowledge and competence in many areas, time and again, including successfully marketing a small independent hotel property that was dwarfed in stature and profile by other well-known national luxury brands.

The typical barbarian is not trusted because his staff and employees tend to view their arrogance as self-serving. We knew that Fred certainly had an outsized ego, but we also knew he wasn't driven exclusively by his self-interests. That is why we believed in him. If he was confident, demanding, and obsessive, we viewed those behaviors in the context of his better underlying qualities.

For these reasons, Fred is my evil genius, but with a small "e."

Chapter 7

⚋⚋⚋

TWELVE YEARS AND
BEGGING FOR GRACE

*"The moment we cry in a film is not when things are sad
but when they turn out to be more beautiful than we expected them to be." — Alain de Botton*

WE SELDOM KNOW what lies inside of people. The people we see every
day—the quiet young man in the middle office, the intern who forces
a smile, or the forgetful woman—they appear oddly disconnected from
their associates. They are a few of the eighteen percent of workers reported by the Harvard Medical School who are affected by at least a
moderate degree of psychological incapacity in any month.[vii]

The Center for Workplace Mental Health estimates that forty percent of workers experience excessive anxiety in their daily lives. More
than fifty percent of these workers say the inability to manage their
impairment affects their performance, the quality of work, and relationships with coworkers. Over seventy-five percent report that their
failure to adequately govern their emotions harms their relationships

outside of the office.*viii*

We are conditioned from our first jobs to leave personal problems at home. Our places of work can be highly competitive. Therefore, work-related relationships take on a transactional feel where people hide their vulnerabilities from colleagues. For the affected employee, that is what they fear the most—the inability to express their feelings, leading to further estrangement. Perhaps the office is the only safe place they can land. Nevertheless, if their impairment affects productivity to the point of diminishing returns, they become a business liability. Without insight that leads to behavioral change, the individual is trapped in an endless loop of misfortune.

Twelve years had passed, and he wondered how life happened so quickly. Jeremy, already in his middle 30s, lost almost everything and everybody. The upwardly mobile career, the promise of success, the bright future, and the dreams of a stable home in a quiet suburb were gone.

The vitality and toughness he inherited from his father equipped him for the dawn to dusk days. He defined himself by the work he did, but he stopped being that person when his pieces misaligned. It was a loss of identity that left profound emptiness, a sense of the loss of opportunity, and of the distinct components that were important to him—his role in life, his beliefs, and his interests.

His chosen work was hospitality management, which ironically involved engaging people, administering to personal needs, and resolving conflict. However, in his ravaged state, he *was* the conflict, and he couldn't manage himself, his actions, or his reactions. Under such conditions, maintaining meaningful employment was nearly impossible because repeated malfunction is a self-reinforcing concept.

It was a slow descent to the dark and unforgiving place. In the summer of 1997, Jeremy was living with her, not because he chose to, but because he surrendered to life's circumstances. For years, the undiagnosed disease did all it could, and he would rather be with someone than be alone. The broken person doesn't find an unbroken one. The laws of attraction and momentum work both ways. So it was another ill-advised relationship which would undoubtedly end with personal wreckage. All his relations in recent years ended the same way because their foundations sat precariously on old, unhealed fault lines. It was a sad testimonial to the compelling need for physical human contact, even in the absence of a genuine and meaningful connection.

Jeremy knew he didn't belong there. But the illness reduces choices, and in the free fall of despair, he couldn't see a clear path ahead. The disease is a thief of the present and future, and it hijacked his ability to make the correct, but difficult decision to leave. It was pulling him back, forcing him to retreat to a more comfortable mind space to avoid the inevitable anxiety that would have accompanied his departure from the relationship. However, his damaged psyche wouldn't let him relinquish the few comforts he had left. That is the irony of the ailment. It builds a false firewall of perceived safety. It makes its victims act against their best interests, resistant to the very knowledge and strategies to help the mind become healthy.

We become what we do, with an innate capacity to internalize and normalize disappointment and failure, the same as success and achievement. At least Jeremy's work had always been an oscillating barometer of his self-worth. But with his confidence in shambles, he engineered the trifecta of personal catastrophe—the loss of meaningful relationships, employment, and the creature comforts of his own home. His life became a minefield of missteps seemingly controlled by an evil puppeteer who laughed at his misdeeds, reducing his existence to a primitive fight for survival. He kept telling himself that someday, his circumstances would change. Although someday was never today.

Raised on inner-city asphalt with middle-class swagger, he was 200 lbs. of mostly muscle and bone. It was embarrassing to confront feelings of powerlessness in a society that glorifies composed, courageous, and rugged men. He was naturally unassuming and modest, but the disease isolated him, making him exceedingly uncomfortable in his skin, unable to feel the warmth of another human being. At times, he couldn't carry on a normal conversation or make eye contact with his associates. He turned away from a fixed gaze as a prizefighter recoils from blows coming his way. Unexplained and generalized pain from the free flow of cortisol through his body became a natural way to feel. Weary by the battle raging inside of him, he was impossible to confront, and he became someone he barely recognized—an objectionable and unlovable human being—angry, sullen, and joyless.

Damaged people tend to act erratically, and the effort to rid himself of unresolved mental conflict resulted in anger directed at others in a desperate attempt to find inner peace. Coworkers couldn't see his emptiness, but they recognized his behavior, which became increasingly obnoxious. His fitful demeanor was fertile ground for a life of future misjudgments that grew like compounded negative interest and sent him spiraling into the waiting arms of emotional quicksand.

Clinical depression is a deadly chameleon that doesn't telegraph its arrival. Like the reflection in a funhouse mirror, it curves and distorts reality as the brain's wounded neurotransmitters desperately seek stable ground. It bobs, weaves, and shifts with time. Like the alien force in *The Predator* movie, it is a master of misperception. It mutates, transforms, and reveals different shades of itself to keep its victim off balance and in perpetual confusion.

Without the awareness that leads to behavioral change, the disease continues to confound and disorient its victim. Some say it feels like a beloved pet has died—every day. It is an illness of chronic sorrow that pounds the soul and renders it to stone, resulting in psychological detachment, sequestering the mind until it withdraws from society. What undivided consciousness is left builds a protective shell, a wall, to shield itself from elevated stress levels and anxiety—the mind saving itself.

It is a disease of feelings, and we can't explain what we don't feel. The mind and body are interconnected, so the loss of ability to feel extends to the physical being too. Victims of depression describe a loss of tactile sensation. Food tastes bland and uninteresting. They stop smelling flowers. Beautiful music no longer moves them.

The disease narrows the perception of the world and represses the ability to see events as they are, like seeing the world through a dirty windowpane. But the afflicted person doesn't know their very existence is lying to them since they can only relate their experience through the shadows of heightened anxiety that ravages the brain's messaging center. Therefore, the mind cannot successfully accumulate separate pieces of information to form vital bridges of nuanced thinking, which embraces good judgment and different perspectives. That is the foundation of interpersonal conflict, both personal and professional, for many people who experience depression. Runaway emotions rule the day when there is an absence of an accurate interpretation of life's events.

In life, ideas form character, or how we operate in the world. We become what we think we are. In the throes of the illness, angry inner thoughts reflect in external actions. The injured psyche fights for survival and engages in acts contrary to the very things it needs to remedy itself instead of stepping toward the light where healing can begin.

Jeremy tried to conquer his devil by living a life of misplaced values, an illusory existence of excess, relentlessly pursuing money, possessions, and accolades. Sufferers of depression go to great lengths to feel human, and he spent too many nights in strange places hoping to relieve the wretched isolation of emotional numbness. It is a circular model of personal destruction—the ball and chain of daily existence, weighing down and exhausting its victim. A cure is solely dependent upon its victim's recognition of irregular, intangible symptoms that are grievously confusing.

Jeremy kept so many failures from his parents. He was a grown man, and he wouldn't ask for a handout. He had to heal himself and repair the injury created by his mismanagement of life's forces. Still, if anything were left, it was the fierce protective instincts he inherited from his father. People fight and die over the preservation of dignity, and it was the only thing the illness didn't take from him. Not on that night in August 1997.

On that warm evening, his head felt heavy in his hands as recurring notions of regret occupied him, pulling him into his past. Raised to be proud and independent, he couldn't stop thinking about how he arrived at this forsaken place. His living condition of semi-dependency created a self-loathing that pierced his pride. With his survival at risk, he grew accustomed to settling for life's low common denominators, taking the safest alternatives to avoid more anxiety.

Then the phone rang at 5:40 p.m. as he was preparing to leave to work at a friend's restaurant. He was moonlighting since his work credentials, once a source of pride, became a tangle of lost opportunity and short tenures. The call was from Ron, a recruiter he recently met. He barely knew Ron, but Ron asked him if he had a desire to go home. The phone call meant he could be close to family and the few friends he had left.

With her sitting beside him, Jeremy hesitated, bewildered by the words on the other end of the phone. It was all so strange to him because lifelines always seemed far away, existing only in his imagination, made for others, but not for him. His tangled synapses wouldn't let him believe he was worthy of such a kind fate. But the disease was there too, bellowing, screaming that he wasn't deserving of good fortune that suddenly fell like manna from the heavens.

While straining and fighting through a labyrinth of confusing emotions, he sensed an unfamiliar feeling of a new resolution. He found his voice and said yes, he would go. By the random happenstance of an unexpected call, he found the strength to face down the monster that bedeviled him for so long. For the first time, he had the clarity of purpose to be unbothered by the hurt in her eyes. Her silence said she knew he had to go. She probably knew he would never get better if he stayed.

When the phone rang that evening, it was as if a force outside of him, perhaps above him, said that he had enough. As much as the disease tried to manipulate him, telling him not to venture into the unknown, he could sense that kinder and gentler footprints lie ahead, making tracks for him to follow. Perhaps the someday he longed for was indeed today.

It didn't take long before he packed a suit and traveled the following day to meet with the vice president. Indeed, he needed the funds, but it wasn't about the money. What he needed most were the soft goods, the immaterial things one acquires when they are a fully functioning and working member of society—recognition, touch, community, status, validation, joy, and the satisfaction that comes from personal accomplishment.

It was the most peculiar interview he ever experienced. For about sixty minutes, the vice president occupied him, told him of the business's unique positioning in the group's portfolio and the company's plans for growth and expansion. Oddly, the interviewer didn't ask Jeremy about his credentials or his recent tattered work history. But the disease is sinfully magnificent, and it was there too, lurking in the shadows, circling its prey, sending signals to Jeremy's mind that he didn't belong there.

The illness thrives in the turmoil of personal disorder. It wanted to pull Jeremy back behind his false wall. So he strained with whatever unbroken consciousness he had left to remain in the moment. Fighting the urge to oversell, he struggled to say less and to remember not to trust the unfiltered words that might tumble from his injured psyche. The meeting seemed to wrap up inconclusively, and it left him confused. While trying to hide his quiet desperation, he summoned the strength to poke the elephant in the room. He asked if they were hiring him. They said they were.

Jeremy left the interview feeling disoriented because serendipitous things didn't happen to him. The brain's primitive reward center that controls acceptance, recognition, and love was in a pitched battle with the contrary impulses of the disease. He couldn't allow himself to feel elated because he had internalized disappointment for so long. The illness was calling him again, telling him it must be a cruel prank, engineered by the minister of the minefield, the evil puppeteer he knew so well. He had to get to a telephone immediately and verify with Ron that this turn of events wasn't a distortion created by his unstable mind. In an era before cell phones, the hour it took him to get to his parents' home seemed like an eternity.

Still unsure if he should believe his good fortune, he was stunned when Ron said those sixty minutes were not an interview—they were an orientation. He hung up the phone and collapsed with emotion. His wall finally crumbled. It was long enough since someone was kind to him and too long since he felt the warmth of blind trust and acceptance. Little did these two individuals know, these two strangers—Ron and the vice president—that they perhaps saved a life that day. On that day, the disease didn't win.

The tears that came freely were of joy and respite and providence. They were tears of newfound weightlessness and gratitude, as he realized that a force was watching over him, keeping him safe all those years. They were the tears of surrender and profound awakening. He remembers that he slept soundly that night for the first time in years, finally knowing an angel was always on his shoulder.

Then a few good things began to happen. Jeremy was away from the town he grew to dislike because it reminded him of so much failure. But now he was in familiar, comfortable surroundings, and an extraordinary sense of calm came over him on the day he began his new assignment. The rage that consumed most of his adult life began to dissipate. It was ushered in years before, by a single episode that ripped open the soft underbelly of his psyche and overwhelmed his coping mechanisms. It was defeated twelve years later by a flickering in time, a chance encounter with a stranger who was randomly scrolling his Rolodex.

On that day, Jeremy felt a pensiveness and thoughtfulness he hadn't known in years. There was an awkward bounce in his step, almost as if he was gliding on a cushion of air. For once, the wind was beneath him and not in front of him. He felt his soul begin to rise, and his senses come alive. His body, his sense of touch, wanted to know all it missed. While other people ran to seek cover from the rain, he enjoyed walking through it because he yearned for the long, lost connection with nature.

He felt a remarkable sensation of serenity as his perceptions of the world began to change. They seemed so much more vivid and brilliant. Like drawing curtains back to reveal a glorious morning sun, he transcended a state of profound and unrelenting darkness to an awakening of humanity that was so much more normal and authentic. For twelve years, he begged for grace. It would come, and with it, a world that was indeed a beautiful place.

The great psychologist Abraham Maslow once said that a single glimpse of heaven is enough to confirm its existence.

He believes that. And, so do I.

We maintain a tight-lipped workforce. The stigma of mental illness is real. Less than half of the affected workers share information with a supervisor or a colleague. There is the fear of being labeled weak and unfit for future promotion, or just misunderstood as someone unwilling to do the required work. No one wants to be the subject of water-cooler whispering about being crazy. Nevertheless, it remains a $44 billion liability for American employers in lost productivity and excessive absenteeism due to a range of disorders. The Integrated Institute of Benefits has a much higher number of over $100 billion.[ix]

There have been instances when I noticed something different about an employee. On each of these occasions, it didn't take long for the employee to dissolve once I helped them connect a few dots. While the manifestations of impairment are unnoticed or undetected by most, the symptoms are less confusing to me. In most of these encounters, the affected worker is in a fight to maintain their equilibrium. They are fearful that their problems will affect their work and their future employment.

In the depressive episode, there is a change in the ability to think and to process information, resulting in poor judgment and diminished decision-making skills. That is the behavioral change that is evident to office associates—the effects of declining mental acuity. Even after the depression has lifted, the aftereffects, or PTSD, can linger because the brain's amygdala—its processor of memory, emotion, anger, fear, and sadness—remains active. Therefore, victims of clinical depression can carry their behavior with them. That is at least one of the reasons we see intelligent and talented individuals fail to maintain stable employment.

The scenery may change. But without the awareness that leads to a permanent, contextual shift in identity and renewed consciousness, the behavior does not.

Chapter 8

SIMON, STAR OF THE
TRAVELING MEDICINE SHOW

*Traveling Medicine Show — A touring act that peddled
"miracle cures" and other products between various en-
tertainments. Common in the United States in the nine-
teenth century, especially in the Old West, these shows
usually promoted miracle elixirs, sometimes referred to as
"snake oil."*

A SNAKE SHEDS its skin two-to-four times per year to allow for future
growth. Simon, master of the instant metamorphosis, had different
skins for investors, employees, senior managers, vendors, and customers. He possessed a talent for hyperbole, making things sound better
or worse than they were. Some would say it was a smoke-and-mirrors
technique so thoroughly practiced it should have landed him on the
wrong side of prison bars, or at least in a civil court of law.

His first foray into entrepreneurship came as a teenager, at least by his admission. He said he sold furniture, the furniture that was in his house. He said his parents were absent, so he decided it was a convenient opportunity for a garage sale. They returned to a sparsely furnished home. Assuming the story is true, Simon sowed the seeds of manipulation and borderline sociopathology at a young age. As a teen, he learned that he could profit if people were inclined to give him the benefit of their doubt.

Encouraged and excited by his successful entrée into the business world, he later, supposedly, segued in and out of various businesses at a dizzying pace, gliding seamlessly from one enterprise to another. At different times in his young life, and depending on one's level of credulity, he was a fashion designer, marketing consultant, filmmaker, magazine publisher, interior designer, model, talent agency owner, and finally, a restaurateur. He claimed to have built twenty-one restaurants among thirty startups, which is impossible to verify since none of the businesses appear to have existed for more than a year or two.

Simon certainly didn't have the outward manifestations of the self-proclaimed, confident Renaissance man he wanted to be. He usually dressed in the same denim jeans and a flowing white, untucked shirt. He had a habit of jamming his hands in his front pockets while shuffling about with his eyes perpetually cast down. A body language expert might say he was hiding a deficiency.

A ghost is difficult to see and harder to catch, and Simon moved in a netherworld of flimsy LLCs, DBAs, and shell companies. The "medicine" he sold undoubtedly existed. Bricks and mortar were there for all to see. Unfortunately, it never worked for more than a short time. He was enamored with the dream, the chase of success, but he wasn't made for the grind. What he built with another person's money, their misplaced faith, or both wasn't sustainable.

He was a visionary in the business of dreams. As a showman, he sold imagery, a vision of grandeur and spine-tingling anticipation that was difficult to ignore. Buyers purchase with emotion, and Simon was an accomplished manipulator of hope. He knew there was a profound distinction between what buyers needed and what they wanted, and he was skilled at selling desire. However, Simon had a practiced formula. He sold his glitzy plans to unsuspecting capitalists who saw a restaurant as a showcase, an adult playpen full of entertainment, action and moving bodies.

When investors fund someone's dream, they also purchase their good faith, history, and knowledge. In most business relationships, there is a natural presumption, a hopeful standard of reliability that precedes the sale. Simon was magnificent at exploiting the suspension of disbelief, the idea that buyers don't assume the worst outcome. They make decisions based on information that is available to them at the time. The difference here is that Simon controlled the script. He sold goods and ideas based on his history or his story of supposed past successes that were impossible to authenticate. It is within these margins where Simon operated. Once he had possession of someone else's money, it became a license to play any way he chose.

Gerald was ready to depart an iconic dining institution after the low-hanging, ripened fruit of new challenges dried up. He was no longer satisfied with maintaining what he helped to build. He wanted new objectives, and boredom is a powerful motivator. He had the stability and expertise from years managing hundreds of employees under challenging circumstances at luxury venues. If Simon could add Gerald and others like him to his growing stable, it would bolster his business credibility—or his ego. Simon planned to have five restaurants. What he offered was the exciting work Gerald wanted to do from a higher perch, like future site selections, project management, business and concept development, and lease negotiations.

Shortly after arriving, it didn't take long for Gerald's antenna to rise after watching Simon move cash around like in a shell game. John the accountant, a thoughtful and industrious man, also questioned his recent decision to leave his previous employer to work for Simon. John called Gerald before his arrival to the company to express his reservations with Simon's business practices. However, the wheels were already in motion, and they both sensed that Simon sold them a less-than-honorable bill of goods.

It was within Gerald's purview to evaluate talent and hire the right people within the constraints of an operating plan. Simon, however, was fascinated with the idea of window dressing his latest toy, making whimsical decisions without advice or consent from those who were supposed to save him from himself. As a self-described impresario, he believed his budding restaurant kingdom needed a celebrity chef, or perhaps a celebrity host. He hired them at outrageous sums of money, believing them to be the missing magical piece of his up-and-coming empire. The problem was that consumers rarely dine out to see an expensive host or a favorite chef, the types Simon believed were his saviors.

It is unethical, but not criminal, when an operator irresponsibly spends investment capital like Monopoly money for the sole purpose of self-enrichment. Although for Simon, two plus two never equaled four. It equaled whatever he wanted.

Shrewd and practiced restaurateurs build for sustainability, knowing the demand for their product is arbitrary. They don't only sell food and beverage. They sell an image, a brand. They sell a style that brings people to their door. However, it is the totality of the experience and all supporting pieces in alignment that entices them to return. But Simon's expertise was limited to the show, anticipating that style and emotion would sell itself.

The few professionals Simon hired, including Gerald, hoped Simon knew enough to get out of their way. But Simon wasn't content to stand by and allow others the freedom to operate to a prescribed plan. He was the narcissistic curator of his carefully created universe. He played with the levers and tools of operations, inserting himself into everyday situations despite the processes his team desperately tried to put in place. As someone said, Simon involved himself in things just enough to screw them up.

Soon, it was painfully clear that it was never Simon's intention to partner with those he hired to run his business. They existed exclusively to help him facilitate his self-interests. After all, if Simon let them run the company, their decisions would have been at odds with his desire to live mainly on the backs of his unwitting financiers until he could no longer sustain the dubious bill of goods he sold them.

Beware the businessman with thousands of social media friends. That is someone, like Simon, who has a relationship base a mile wide, but only an inch deep. People are the tools of the hospitality trade, and vital and stable relations are its driving force. Firm relationships with staff members, vendors, and customers are of equal importance. These relationships must be interconnected like a choreographed dance and nurtured to build trust and consistency. It is improbable, if not impossible, that such associations can contribute in any meaningful way if they are all viewed as throwaway entities, a mere body count. For Simon, employees and vendors were as disposable as bar straws.

Under these circumstances, Gerald's relationship with Simon lasted barely a few months. Simon sold his tales of grandeur to many people who allowed emotions and dreams of prosperity to influence their better judgment. In a heightened state of anticipation, the world can seem like a better place. It is easy to be lured into a dream-like state when confronted with a new and exciting opportunity. It is natural to feel exhilarated when presented with an occasion to be appreciated and rewarded. Except, it remains infinitely more challenging to train the mind to remove emotion by contemplating not just what riches lie ahead, but the associated risk as well.

Simon wasn't an evil boss in an archetypal manner. More closely related to an opportunist, he was the nonthreatening center of his universe. Ever the showman, it was all theatre, and he was the lead character who didn't know when to exit the stage. Responsible owners, using the servant leadership model, pay their employees and suppliers first. They work to serve others. As unmindful as he was, Simon put himself first, even if it meant his employees' checks bounced, and he wasn't paying his partners and vendors who were demanding cash on delivery, money he didn't have.

The beleaguered chef, unable to purchase food from his mainline supplier, was forced to shop at local grocery stores using his credit cards while hoping for reimbursement. Employees can generally understand the peaks and valleys of business. They realize that demand is subjective. However, they will never understand when the company's failure and the subsequent effect on their lives are squarely on the shoulders of an owner who mismanages obligations and pays themself first or purchases expensive toys at their expense.

Simon operated in arrears knowing people needed jobs, and they would most likely remain in his employ if he owed them wages. For Simon, the best employee was one waiting for a paycheck. It was free labor, and he could keep them lingering in anticipation until the doors closed, and the medicine show took to the road again.

He repeated the formula many times over. It was under these circumstances that Simon, the merchant peddler, inevitably failed. As untrue to himself as he was, he rationalized to potential future investors by saying he had a great business idea, but an unlucky location. It was a self-patented formula, although it wasn't a real system with plans, metrics, or analytics. His method was merely a patina, a sales pitch he had burnished from adolescence.

If Simon did build twenty-one restaurants, none exist today. Still, I am sure it is a number that makes him proud. Anyone would want to say they built twenty-one of anything. Assuming the number is correct, it was equally tragic in its sheer, sorcerous scope of deception. It meant Simon sold twenty-one investors on a bill of goods he was unable to deliver. Twenty-one sets of hard-working employees, hundreds of them, had their lives disrupted. Twenty-one teams of dedicated managers didn't bring home paychecks, and twenty-one landlords and dozens of honest vendors didn't receive compensation for their good faith, goods, or services.

The sad reality is that shattering livelihoods through inept or unethical business practices is not a crime. No statute prevents an inept businessperson from selling hopeful sponsors and workers on a dream that becomes a nightmare through incompetence or gross mismanagement. Perhaps there is a civil liability. However, it is rarely worth anyone's effort to sue a ghost in a court of law.

It was appropriate that Simon eventually wound up living on a friend's sofa, broke and alone. The traveling medicine show finally came to a halt, collapsing under its weight. Ultimately, the most persuasive schemer can run out of victims and other people's money.

Simon's formula was the work of a highly skilled and motivated manipulator. After all, to be able to build a house of cards twenty-one times is nothing short of magnificent. Perhaps it was magnificent. But it was a perversion of grandness, a wicked testimonial to the perseverance and staying power of a sociopath.

Chapter 9

———∾∾———

MADDIE, MISTRESS OF THE SCORCHED EARTH

"The amount of times you say you hate drama is directly proportional to the amount of times you actually start it."
— Unknown

JASON NEVER KNEW anyone who could induce such a torrent of collective eye-rolling exasperation. Maddie was a magnificently made diva, walking through space with an air of spectacular indifference—a genuine Mistress of the Scorched Earth. She talked about her coworkers as if they didn't exist while they sat six feet away. Her eyes were either semi-permanently cast down or glued to the ceiling from rolling them at her not-so-hidden disdain of an associate. Through pursed lips, she showed contempt for others who didn't meet her specific criterion of approval.

Although helpful to some people, she was insulting, snarky, and uncooperative to others. Prickly sensitive, she expected perfection from everyone, except herself. Well-practiced at dissecting everyone's words and actions, however benign or innocent, she never passed an opportunity to express outrage. Not given her due, she was quick to let others know just how unenlightened they were.

We almost have begrudging envy for the celebrity diva, the one with the gravitas to demand Beluga caviar flown in from a corner of the globe so they can have a midnight snack with their teacup comfort dog. However, the image of Meryl Streep in *The Devil Wears Prada* comes to mind when you hear of a workplace diva. We connect with her character because she is more real than the red-carpet performance diva we see from media images filmed from behind wooden barricades. Streep's diva type usually exists in media, print, film, entertainment, and fashion. They have the power and position to be able to produce and control what we see, hear, wear, and read. They are the creators and drivers of our culture.

Still, we would never confuse the Streep diva with Maddie, the more common workplace diva-barbarian most of us encounter. When a diva such as the Streep character occupies a higher position, it can indeed be frustrating for colleagues and coworkers. At least, over time, their actions become more predictable, and the office associates know there is little choice except to indulge and manage the diva's demands. But when the diva is equal, it is easy to grow resentful of the ingrained histrionics and useless high drama, which wastes time and energy.

Maddie was a narcissist but in reverse. Narcissists blow hot air into a room, while she pulled it out. If the true narcissist is an expert at creating feelings of inadequacy in those around them, she was equally skilled at creating resentment by her sheer audacity and the naked presumption that everyone should recognize her sensitivities. And be aware of the diva with hurt feelings. Her feelings were always hurt, creating a perpetual atmosphere of agitation for those around her. It was her natural state of being.

Completely self-absorbed, Maddie saw the world through very narrow optics. Because she moved in a self-styled existence of perpetual victimhood, she was always the bullied one, but never the bully.

Unfortunately, that qualified almost everyone else as a bully, too un-kind for her eternally offended sensibilities. However, she was a bully in her own right. If the definition of a bully is someone who seeks to exert undue influence over others through intimidation, she was un-doubtedly a bully. Her weapon of choice was just more subtle—a self-diagnosed, enduring psychological injury suffered from the destructive words and actions of others.

There were few light-hearted moments with Maddie. In her pres-ence, the room usually fell silent, the mood suddenly heavy with dread. Clipped and carefully crafted soundbites replaced the usual free and typical banter among workplace acquaintances who spent more time with each other than loved ones. They had to make sure their spoken words passed through Maddie's uber-thin filter. Jason's typical workday was stressful enough but tasked with managing the fleeting fancy of the self-righteous diva, the day was downright exhausting.

Diva office dynamics are not unlike other workplace theatrics. Selectively deferential, they decide the parameters of the relationship with their superiors. It is the diva who decides if they get along or not. It all depends on what the diva is permitted to get away with. The more compliant supervisor is a friend. A boss who sees through and holds the diva accountable will be an enemy. Although the diva will usually tread more lightly with the boss, they are a hand-flipping, over-the-shoulder mumbling menace to others.

Interestingly, divas usually accept their superiors if they are the one who enters a new culture. In that situation, they have little choice but to assimilate. They may step more softly and have a tinge of gratitude since they were taken in by a new family. However, if a fresh-faced boss enters an environment where a diva reigns supreme with deeply embedded negative behaviors, the boss has unknowingly signed up for a ready-made minefield of emotional mayhem.

Unfortunately, Maddie was the beneficiary of previous bosses. They decided she was worth keeping despite a lengthy history of un-seemly and shameless attempts to push limitations and manipulate every opportunity to her economic advantage. Insatiable greed can be a most unattractive quality, and Maddie never perceived her offensive actions, or hostile reactions, to be anything more than business as usual. She became what she was permitted to become.

Later, she was diagnosed with a severe illness. She returned to work, but not before her problem became everyone else's. Her condition required substantial treatment. Regrettably, it also provided the perfect set of circumstances for her to attempt to muster sympathy above and beyond what she already thought she was most deserving. It was easy for her to believe that what she desired was what she was entitled to. If there was an added dosage of compassion for her, it was quickly lost in the ether of her heightened victim status.

Jason had the keys to the building's mechanical systems. It was an old structure that, over the years, became a hodge-podge of cooling and heating Band-Aids, which were obsolete and ineffective. A single-zone system tempered the air in the building's office space, designed to work for multiple workstations. Therefore, what was a comfortable environment for one team member was distressing for another.

The daily battle raged on with some employees claiming heatstroke, while others asserted to suffer from sub-normal body temperatures. As the building manager, Jason maintained that it is more practical to warm oneself when chilled as opposed to cooling when uncomfortably hot. This concept is called putting on a sweater. Unfortunately, that was too pragmatic for Maddie, who claimed her condition left her in a state of malignant hypothermia. The hypothermia persisted as soon as the ambient temperature dropped below seventy-five degrees. True to her form, she made it Jason's fault since he had the keys to the controls, and if he desired, he could alleviate her extreme discomfort by sliding the little red needle to the right to provide more heat. It didn't take long for her to claim she was deliberately frozen out, the victim of a callous and hostile environment; and it was Jason's evil plan to exacerbate her condition and force her out of the company.

One strategy to effectively deal with a diva is to give her a taste of her tonic and, at least momentarily, become a demon to fight the devil. Never one to let an opportunity for stinging sarcasm pass, Jason offered to burn down the building, and, in the embers, he'd sacrifice a couple of live animals. He'd then run a marathon while saying an Act of Contrition at church. That would certainly fix the frightful and abhorrent existence the diva suffered through every day.

From the perspective of productivity, a diva can be singularly focused on tasks and tend to be a highly driven and motivated employee. So performance with a diva is rarely an issue. Performance issues are more comfortable to diagnose and to correct. They are tied to measurable results. However, individual behavior is much more abstract and challenging to manage. Although the real issue with a diva is they don't see themselves as a diva. With a deeply ingrained sense of importance, their self-entitlement is impenetrable, thus immune to the insight which makes humility and mindfulness attainable.

When faced with a challenge involving personnel, smart leaders want to look for business reasons to be corrective. Unfortunately, the diva doesn't usually provide the boss with a business reason to act. In the case of the diva, there isn't necessarily a perceptible loss of opportunity. Their behavior doesn't manifest itself transparently on a balance sheet or a quarterly statement. In that regard, they are as threatening as other difficult personalities.

Nevertheless, the other associates are looking to the boss to rectify the diva behavior or any other barbarian type because it affects their morale and culture. The manager must juggle competing synergies and emotions while fighting battles on multiple fronts at the risk of appearing weak and feeble. In the meantime, the office energy shifts from creativity to damage control. Even in a right-to-work state, the boss usually can't fire the diva-barbarian to satisfy the other workers' bloodlust, no matter how legitimate those emotions are.

Still, divas possess star attributes, and their managers often give them the benefit of the doubt. They receive favorable judgment because they usually react disproportionately when confronted. The process can take weeks or months of proper documentation to prove or demonstrate the harmful effects of the diva. However, if the boss doesn't take definitive action, there is enough of an opening for a torch-and-pitchfork faction to rise. It is a matter of carefully navigating the process to everyone's ultimate satisfaction.

So, the manager has choices to make. They can try to maintain a positive relationship with the diva. Perhaps the boss can't control them, but they can attempt to hold them to the same expectations. If the boss keeps the diva, others will notice that they must have clear and decisive business reasons for doing so. Finally, the manager can decide if the collateral damage is worth the price of ransom. In my experience, it usually isn't.

Maddie was rarely part of the communal culture. Rather than assisting in bringing the team together, she pulled it apart because she decided for herself which boundaries to observe. Her happiness was rooted in her ability to manipulate people and events to her satisfaction. She had lofty expectations of how others should behave to facilitate her comfort, and she secretly punished associates who fell short of her criterion. Her passive-aggression took the form of malicious gossip, designed to diminish the standing of the offenders or to orchestrate their demise through a campaign of manufactured defamation.

Her ability to shape circumstances was a result of a deeply seated conviction of moral superiority. She was an expert at dangerously stage-managing emotions to her advantage, shifting seamlessly, effortlessly, between sniveling petulance and maudlin syrupy sweetness.

She eventually left the company when her gravy train of privilege came to a halt. She enjoyed the benefit of undue riches from feeble and clueless enablers, unwilling to do the hard work of holding her accountable for her destructive behavior. It took years until others, fresher faces, finally decided they could no longer endure her gluttonous entitlement.

Not unexpectedly, she ruthlessly scorched the earth during her exit interview. She spared no one because, to her mind, there wasn't a team member with a redeeming quality—save the few who advanced her agenda to behave like an institution of one.

In the end, she did what came naturally to her. She picked up her toys and weapons, and went home.

Chapter 10

RECKONING ON A ROOFTOP

"I have been driven many times upon my knees by the overwhelming conviction that I had nowhere else to go. My own wisdom and that of all about me seemed insufficient for that day." — Abraham Lincoln

ON THE EVENING of December 22, 2001, he was alone on a rooftop. In one hand was a bottle, and in the other, it was the rest of his life. He had a simple choice to make.

It was almost twenty years of the hopeless and self-immolating desolation of alcoholism, addiction, self-loathing, and self-abuse. He was barely thirty years old. He knew that unless he were where the monster wasn't, his life would never be more than a series of late-night benders that were slowly destroying his young internal organs.

Ironically, that lofty place in the sky was his bottom. Tired of being sick and tired, he chose life. He decided to stop fighting that he was a hopeless alcoholic. He resolved to accept that all that had happened up to that time occurred for a reason. He chose life because he knew there had to be more to it than lying on his apartment floor, shaking with hallucinations, begging to be set free. He chose life because he knew he had to have a more meaningful existence, one released from the death-grip of desperation and hopelessness of alcoholism. Through the haze of his wasted mind, he chose life because he knew there was enough left to live since the ten-year-old boy in him stopped living all those years ago.

The disease is a prolific liar, and it makes its host victims magnificent liars. One must be an exceptional liar to convince adult onlookers, perhaps teachers and coaches, to suspend their disbelief about the young addict's pathetic living condition. One must be a prodigious liar to be able to assure oneself they can quit at any time. Addiction is a crafty combatant. It is one of the handful of diseases that tells the mind it is not ill.

Alcoholism is a "partner" illness, one in which the toxic effects on the wrecked and ravaged mind and body begin to feel usual and customary. It leaves its victim in a progressive state of ruin, which becomes a new normal. We can never be who we are and what we want to be at the same time, and addicts caught in this deadly cycle don't see a world beyond the relentless pursuit of their agent provocateur. Their single-minded and all-consuming quest is a thief of hope, and it defines their present and future.

The vehicle of alcohol works on the brain's primitive reward center of pleasure, safety, and gratification. The incremental consumption of alcohol slowly reduces the rational, cognitive mind's ability to make informed decisions about its limitations. The brain's limbic system—the seat of emotion, behavior, and motivation—reinforced by the mighty hallucinogenic, overpowers the rational mind, which soon capitulates to the more commanding primal need for acceptance. However, the need for approval is not just emotionally driven.

David DiSalvo, the author of *Brain Changer*, explains that the human body is an adaptable machine. As much as alcohol is an inhibitor, it is also an exciter. The consumption of alcohol increases the release of dopamine, the brain's neurotransmitter of pleasure. But it does so artificially, tricking the mind into believing that it is satisfied. The mind then seeks more alcohol to experience more dopamine release. Since the mind and the body are highly efficient and flexible mechanisms, they build a tolerance to the invading outside agent, requiring more consumption of it to reach the desired state of consciousness, or buzz.

At the same time, alcohol alters other brain chemicals, resulting in enhanced feelings of depression. That explains why some abusers exhibit signs of giddiness while others become enraged, violent, sorrowful, or extraordinarily melancholy. Addiction takes hold when the drinker feels the recurring and compulsive need to return to the feeling of dopamine release in the brain's reward center.[x]

He lost his father to a terminal illness at the age of ten. His grandfather tried to assume the role of a surrogate father, only to die barely a year later. At his young age, the heroes in his life, the providers of spiritual sustenance, weren't in abundance, and he lost the only two he had. His mother, overwhelmed with grief, also missed the two most prominent figures in her life. Unable to function in day-to-day life, she was ill-equipped to manage her profound sadness while attending to the demands of raising her two young children.

Emotionally orphaned, he was susceptible to anxiety and antisocial behavior. With adult figures removed from his life, he lost the foundation built on his understanding of the world. He drifted, and drank, and by age thirteen, he wandered in and out of school, sometimes not in attendance for weeks at a time. School letters went to his home only to remain unopened. He drifted from sofa to sofa, basement to basement, and eventually, from one dusty, flophouse floor to another—the kind of places where single bulbs dangle overhead. By sixteen, he was the prototype of the angry, addicted, and aimless teen.

Occasionally, curious adult spectators poked their heads into his life. But morally disengaged strangers only do so much. Most of them shake their heads and feel thankful it isn't their son or daughter who is suffering. There is rarely, if ever, a leader or a savior among passive onlookers. Rationalization occurs when many bystanders assume someone else is doing the heavy lifting. The boy must have somewhere to go, and there must be someone who loves him. Responsibility successfully diffused. Many people are busy with their own lives. Or they assume they are ill-suited to manage the tragedy unfolding before their eyes. After all, every neighborhood has at least one house, one foreboding place, where people know something sinister is going on. They just don't know what to do with the information they have.

Depending on one's point of view, alcoholism is either a disease, a choice, or a result. However, I have yet to meet anyone who would advocate that a thirteen-year-old boy could wantonly choose a path of self-destruction. Choice implies that this boy, who was once recognized and positioned as a gifted child with natural intellectual and athletic prowess, made the rational decision to plan his young life so the alcohol was never too far away. Choice meant his young mind was capable of elaborate planning, astute enough to design opportunities to drink alone, and conscious enough to decide to continue drinking long after others had stopped.

Leaving school was a foregone conclusion, and he dropped out to live life in its margins. Finding solace in the city's music scene, he supported himself by working for quick cash as venue entertainment security. Later he was introduced to the culture of the city's restaurant scene, the equivalent of throwing volatile liquid onto a roaring fire. It turned out to be a perfect fit, but for all the wrong reasons.

A naturally gregarious young man, he loved the restaurant scene and the sense of theatre it provided. Perhaps because he couldn't make himself feel happy, he discovered he had a passion for making other people feel better. He savored the notion that he could have a ringside seat, a glimpse into people's lives in celebration of life's joyous moments since he had so few of them.

He was excited by the free flow of adrenaline associated with the carefully orchestrated, nonstop action of a busy evening with bodies in perpetual motion. And he enjoyed the fact that alcohol was closer than ever. It was close enough that he made the love of fine wine his career. He became a certified sommelier, which meant he could drink the best wines on demand throughout the evening. He must have felt like a wealthy man when he realized he could drink safely on the job. It was a license to steal, and it was entirely usual and customary.

To the casual observer, he appeared to be successful. He had a job he loved in one of the city's most prestigious restaurants. But the restaurant world has a seedy subculture all its own. The constant need to take care of other people and create memorable events for them extends to the memory-makers when the show's curtain closes, and the lights go down.

At the beginning of the evening, there is a feeling of shared purpose among staff members poised for action like the fully compressed spring in a wind-up toy. At the end of the shift, when the spring relaxes, there is a collective team crash as adrenaline levels return to normal. Another night of survival successfully managing the dozens of moving pieces of controlled chaos means there can be a cooperative pat on the back for a job well done. For many, it becomes a nightly tradition, and alcohol, the proxy of social spontaneity, the essential ingredient of ritualistic group decompression, is there for the taking.

That is how it starts. However, on too many occasions, the party continues elsewhere into the wee hours. The process is repeated many times over in restaurants across the land. What begins as a benign celebration soon becomes a recipe for the creation of many more walking corpses than it ever should. Many restaurants and bars exist on the late-night depravities of their industry cohorts enjoying the release of their shadow selves, their darker side. This ritual is ready-made fodder for the addict who is driven by weaker impulses. It combines their primitive need for group identification with their lust for the seductive and intoxicating potion.

Silently, he feared there wasn't a way to work in the city's restaurant scene without engaging in its culture of alcohol abuse. He told himself that drinking was part of his job. The routine was deeply ingrained, and the social pressure to continue can be a powerful motivator since he didn't know anyone who didn't drink. Restaurants have long been cultures of camaraderie. It wasn't unusual to walk into his restaurant at eleven a.m., and the topic of conversation was how many shots were consumed the previous evening. Nevertheless, he was a raging, functioning alcoholic years in the making, and he was dying.

On November 5, 2001, the owner summoned him to the office. He was fearful that his boss knew just how sick he was. He was right. They gave him a choice to enter a rehabilitative facility immediately or clean out his desk. He fumed, and he argued. He said he could quit drinking whenever he wanted. They all say that, and with the effects of addiction fully metastasized, his mind was a whirlwind of conflicting emotions. His mind and body belonged to the disease, and the illness wanted to speak for him and make an easy decision for him. It was telling him to rage against this new existential threat by having a drink at the corner bar.

Although his young liver was failing, he didn't see a life beyond the one he had because it was all he knew. But at that moment, something extraordinary happened. He flashed back to a couple of days before when he fell on his living room floor, begging for relief from the deeply submerged pain in the core of his body.

Something astonishing was indeed happening. While he wasn't a religious man, he was a spiritual man, and it became clear to him he wasn't on this journey alone. He knew then that someone or something was watching over him, keeping him safe and warm in his darkest hours from all those years ago. At that moment, he found the grace to put his trust and life into the hands of benign and helpful strangers, just a few of many he would meet along the way to restoration and recovery. Ironically, desperation was the gift he needed most.

After six weeks, on December 22, 2001, he returned to the job he loved. But as soon as a bottle of wine was in his hands, he panicked. He began to sweat, and with his pulse racing, he ran to that roof. With the disease still calling him, nipping at his heels, he begged for the wisdom to know if he could survive without alcohol. The illness is funny that way. It is a marvel of paradox, condemning its host to live in contradiction, a pitiable life of degenerate survival. It dares its victim not to live with it, but to try to live without it.

Alone and on the rooftop, it came to him, a most unusual and peaceful awakening. The word *surrender* played over in his mind as he chose the extraordinary serenity that comes with resolution. In one glorious instant, he knew he could let go of the shame that bound him from when he was just a small boy. It was twenty years, and at the lofty place in the sky, he chose to forgive himself.

He chose life.

Often viewed as Purgatory, the restaurant world is where people who need a job go before they have a real job. No formal education is required. It is where workers perform on a stage and depart with a bundle of cash. At 5:30 p.m., the curtain rises, and the show is on. One hundred fifty diners come shuffling in with heightened expectations. It is a volatile cocktail mix of speed, expediency, precision, and emotion.

The ritual, the ceremony of dining out, is an emotional decision before it is a financial one. Some people are there for an occasion. Some are there just for a meal cooked by someone who knows more than they do. Nevertheless, they all come to feel better than they did only ninety minutes earlier. That could be an exceptional burden to place on a group of mostly young working strangers, loosely assembled in a hectic atmosphere, unaccustomed to the more civilized and formal comportment of an office environment.

It is a pressure-cooker existence of six-hundred-degree ovens, roaring fires, burning fuel, sharp instruments used to break bone and animal tissue, heightened expectations, and demanding bosses who leverage whatever tools they have at their disposal. There are volatile customers, narrow lanes of passage, and a precarious choreography of many moving pieces, whereby each one must be successfully linked to another to create one happy customer.

For many, it is a breeding ground for excessive self-medication, where people are slowly dying every night in restaurants across the landscape. Behind the expensive and attractive physical trappings, there is a tragedy playing out. The qualifier of a Shakespearean tragedy is that it is about real people. In this tragedy, there are people addicted and dying in numbers that far exceed the national average.

According to the Federal Substance Abuse and Mental Health Services Administration, the hospitality industry ranks number one for illicit drug and alcohol use. The recent opioid epidemic has only complicated matters. The national average of drug abuse in the workplace is 8.6 percent. In the hospitality industry, the number is 19.1 percent, which far exceeds the Arts and Entertainment industry, its nearest competitor, at 13.7 percent. The national average of alcohol abuse is 6.0 percent. In the hospitality industry, it is 11.5 percent.[xi]

It is an industry that places great emphasis on sustainability, a new stamp of approval on its products. However, it has long had a strained relationship with the sustainability of its greatest asset, its people. The industry is heavily reliant on capitalization but places little emphasis on human capital. Long hours, low wages, and a "shift drink" culture take a toll on employees. Alcohol consumption and its abuse were further cemented into the culture when hotel and restaurant unions began making shift beer for cooks a negotiable benefit.

As a young man growing up in the industry, it was perfectly acceptable for the restaurant owner to decree that I drop what I was doing to obtain a drink order for the kitchen. It occurred several times throughout the evening. By eleven p.m., line cooks were on shaky legs before climbing into their vehicles—several more two thousand-pound dangerous road missiles in the making.

For many users and abusers, the industry is a hotbed of opportunity. It provides a lifestyle, a place where alcohol is everywhere. There is alcohol in kitchens, behind the bar, and squirreled away in dimly lit areas. I routinely found coffee cups masquerading as wine glasses and glasses of water infused with gin or vodka. It was all for employee consumption as they performed their duties. This was after repeated warnings that little mercy would be offered if I were to identify the owner of the beverage. Still, it didn't stop employees who couldn't stop themselves.

That is representative of the cycle of destruction, and the desperate actions employees take to keep themselves balanced during a difficult shift. Even if I should terminate an offender's employment, they could walk out the front door and begin the cycle anew at a place up the street. Few questions are asked since the chances are significant that neighboring restaurants are also insufficiently staffed.

The industry is not good at policing itself. Nor is it good at mentoring those who need it the most. That isn't to disparage the thousands of responsible restaurateurs. They are generally small business owners who are ill-equipped to handle a staff of thirty people, one-third of whom may be addicted to drugs or alcohol, or perhaps are harboring other behavioral deficiencies. The small business owner is left to put in safeguards such as security cameras. Except, cameras only protects their assets and don't address the underpins of detrimental staff conduct, and many would argue that cameras shouldn't.

The spotlight on decadent behavior within the restaurant industry cast a shadow on its culture of bawdiness. The industry has long suffered from the perception, and it wouldn't be inaccurate, that it doesn't put its people first. But now, the industry is paying more attention, not just to addiction relief efforts, but to its unseemly history of contributing to the dangerous behavior of its inhabitants. Support groups like *Ben's Friends* are part of that effort.

Founded in 2016, Ben's Friends is an AA-style support group that aids hospitality workers explicitly. The group's mission is simple: to provide a haven for employees to get or to remain sober. The group has no specific plan, like AA's Twelve Steps. Instead, it allows participants to speak their minds about whatever distresses them. Many of the attendees talk about what facilitated their last drink, or their previous hit. Unsurprisingly, many speak about a specific behavior, perhaps by a chef, a coworker, or an unreasonable customer, that precipitated their last trip to the bottle or their drug dealer. This underscores other common deficiencies among hospitality workers, namely, behavioral weaknesses that first ushered in the death spiral of hopeless addiction.

The 501(c)(3) group has organically increased in size to locations in multiple cities. Its message of nonjudgment is simple. All that is required is a desire to get and to remain sober. It provides comfort in familiarity and the shared bond of acceptance and gratitude to live another day.

Chapter 11

RONALD THE SLOTHFUL

"Whenever there is a hard job to be done, I assign it to a lazy man. He is sure to find an easy way of doing it."
— *Walter Chrysler*

HIS FIRST MEETING after signing on the dotted line should have been an omen of things to come. Joel sat at the bar, and they handed him a voluminous book. There wasn't a discussion of expectations, objectives, or the challenges they hired him to resolve. There wasn't a business briefing or orientation about how his role fit into an already established hierarchy.

In that limited interaction, he learned he would be a creature of the night, working until the wee hours of the morning, every morning. He felt misled, and having relocated from two hundred miles away, he couldn't change what they had decided. He could have protested, although that would have diminished his value and put him on shaky ground with the people who had high hopes.

The first emotion he wanted to feel upon starting in a new place of employment was eager excitement, not the twinge of careless non-disclosure. His mind immediately flashed to younger days when he ran hotel bars that closed at four a.m. It was a disorienting lifestyle he never got used to.

One of the first things he noticed was the eyes. They were dark, soft, lazy, almost lifeless. The man in front of him, Ronald, his demeanor, depending on the point of view, was either perfectly lethargic or naturally laid back. He was a man of few words, and he was difficult to size up. His real motive for doing anything was hard to detect until it became apparent that one of his key objectives was to insulate himself through anonymity. Interacting with him meant to be left wanting more—more communication, engagement, and more substance.

Joel was used to bosses who were transparent, and at least for better or for worse, he always knew where he stood. But mysterious Ronald was different. Outwardly soft-spoken and easy-going with a crooked smile, Ronald was almost dangerously charismatic. It was a style and demeanor he used to draw people into his orbit. At least to Joel, Ronald was the perfect opportunist who surrounded himself with buffers to remain happily disengaged. His even temper and easy-going charm provided the perfect smokescreen.

It was an admirable quality for someone in his position when used for the right reasons. However, Ronald employed it as an instrument toward his main objective, which was to stay disconnected, leaving the heavy lifting to others. He could effortlessly trade one tool for another, slathering on layers of veneer to disarm his corporate bosses, leaving them with the illusion that he was a full participant in the business's day-to-day processes. He was an expert at knowing how to look busy at the right moment.

There is a difference between having a lazy intellect and a lazy mentality. While the lazy intellect is the failure to expand the mind to be curious about the world, it is the lazy mentality that lacks grit, the determination to recognize deficiencies and take definitive action. With the lazy mentality affliction, what breaks usually remains broken.

Although highly intelligent, Ronald would never be mistaken for a passionate, persevering, and driven individual who would spend the necessary energy to form strategic and corrective action plans. Such action demands fierce resolve, will, and decisiveness. It is the difference between being involved in the front end of shortcomings or reacting to them on the backside. For the opportunist like Ronald, initiating action other than for self-preservation, or immediate survival was too much work to endure.

The tendency toward inaction is described in the book *Hide and Seek, The Psychology of Self Deception* by Dr. Neel Burton. Dr. Burton concluded that the lazy mind is a manifestation of a manic defense—the tendency, when presented with uncomfortable thoughts, to distract the conscious mind either with a burst of activity or with the opposite thoughts or feelings. It is the lazy mindset that seeks comfort in what it believes to be the safest option, which is to do nothing rather than face the anxiety that accompanies action or confrontation.[xii]

It was evident that Joel and Ronald had different workplace character profiles. Joel was an energetic, independent, self-starter. However, by his admission, he wasn't always tactful or diplomatic enough, or patient enough, especially in his younger years, to spend precious time navigating what he believed was the nonsensical insecurity or incompetence of those less diligent than he was. But Joel's innate sense of duty and obligation to remain faithful to himself and his work ethic, while admirable, had a downside. He couldn't adjust his way of thinking. Once he decided he was unable to suffer the foolishness and laziness of others by his definition of the terms, he was in the crosshairs, viewed as a selfish outsider.

Joel never knew of a restaurant or hotel that thrived with most of the staff members working two or three days per week. In such a model, very few have a vested interest or an emotional connection to their employer. Without a shared common purpose, it is difficult to instill the coveted essential values of continuity and consistency. Hospitality operations are successful when an act of service is performed repeatedly, perfect practice making perfect execution. From a training perspective, it is infinitely more economical to communicate a message or an expectation to six full-time staff members instead of a dozen part-timers.

For the employee students, skiers, aspiring hockey players, and models, flexibility was their priority, and Joel found them exhausting, if not impossible, to manage effectively. One of his priorities was to flip the broken model and replace the transient staff with more reliable associates. Except there was an obstacle standing in his way. That was Ronald, the last person he expected to reject a plan for a desperately needed overhaul. The exercise of removing marginally productive team members meant work, hard work. It meant retraining and resetting expectations with different individuals. It also meant the present model, designed, and engineered by Ronald, was a failure.

People in authority often mistakenly hold on to failure because they don't want to acknowledge their flawed decisions. It is a strange and counterintuitive thought process, born of an inflamed ego. The primal instinct to be right is powerful. The unmindful manager or boss is at the epicenter of their carefully crafted alternate universe. So the change meant an upheaval of what was psychologically comfortable for Ronald. Still, there was more to come.

Joel had to battle Ronald, but he also had to fight Ronald's anointed ones, his apostles. Through the years, Joel learned to navigate unbecoming behavior from militant union brethren. But this was different. To him, these coworkers were born to walk this earth alone, never to intermingle respectfully with anyone, to live alone, and to work alone. Objectionable, insulting, coarse, and at times uncivil, these were employees with a degree of competence who managed to convince their weak boss that they were worth keeping. Silently, Joel wondered how they all wound up in the same place.

The opportunist rarely survives without a human lining, and they, the apostles, serve that purpose. They are fiercely loyal, usually because their existence is made possible by a sympathetic overseer. By the process of internalization, they view the behavior of the boss as usual and customary. Together, they reinforce each other's actions to form a communal firewall of behavioral dysfunction. To Joel's mind, if the boss, Ronald, was mostly inactive and unaccountable, how could he possibly hold others answerable for their barbaric conduct?

The opportunist is an individual seeking a break, an opening to self-preserve. It became painfully apparent to Joel that Ronald condoned his underlings' improper behavior if they helped advance his agenda to remain comfortable and safe.

War is an arm of politics. Ineffective or insubstantial political diplomacy leads to war. Perhaps not dissimilarly, unresolved conflict in an office environment through weak or ineffective intervention compels workers to declare war on one another when all else has failed. When patience runs its course, pride must be protected. Most people, by nature, are not confrontational. It takes years of self-training, introspection, and practice to learn to be respectfully direct and to acquire the necessary skills to interact productively with peers who see the world in a different dimension. So it didn't help that Joel's growing impatience and dismissive demeanor positioned him as an outsider. And no one likes a strident disrupter.

In Joel's opinion, he was, at least, productively troublesome. However, his untrained ego and inability to align his goals with the company's objectives prevented him from realizing why others didn't see things the way he did. His relationship with Ronald, already on unsteady ground, meant he would rarely benefit from the doubt, no matter how logical or insightful he was about the restaurant's deficiencies.

Peaceful co-existence, although a political theory, if applied to leadership currency, is a concept with its footing in reciprocal respect and esteem that develops over time. It is a policy of competition without conflict among widely different ideologies. But for Joel in his relationship with Ronald, born in the haze of mistrust, it was a foregone conclusion that they would never find a place of mutual appreciation.

He had to admit he failed to successfully manage Ronald by not carefully presenting him with productive resolutions to systemic problems. He also was unable to realize that people in positions of leadership, even those we disagree with, carry a burden many associates will never fully comprehend. They have duties and responsibilities that transcend what may be plain for all to see. The element of forgiveness Joel wanted from his boss was the same quality he was unable to afford Ronald or others. Unable to deftly pivot when necessary, he became part of the problem.

Eventually, Joel joined the fifty percent of workers who don't leave a job or an environment as much as they leave an individual. Nevertheless, he also had to acknowledge that he missed an opportunity to be successful not because of Ronald, but regardless of him. Team members must interact despite differences in style, demeanor, character traits, and priorities. Once Joel set his mind that the environment was dysfunctional by his standard, there was nowhere to go. Human nature is a smart judge of behavior. As much as he found his associates' conduct objectionable, they, in turn, evaluated him by what they saw. They saw an angry and resentful coworker who didn't see himself through his personal looking glass. They wouldn't be incorrect.

Chapter 12

———✺———

SIX HOURS, AND A DAY

"Some people, sweet and attractive, and strong and healthy, happen to die young. They are masters in disguise teaching us about impermanence." — Dalai Lama

PATRICK WANTED TO take him to his doorstep. Although strangely, Anil asked to be dropped off almost a full city block from his residence. Patrick could only watch with curiosity as Anil high stepped his way through twelve inches of freshly fallen snow.

The usually reliable and steady employee I came to know and admire recently seemed difficult to reach. His conversation, often glib and breezy, was clipped, distant, and disengaged. Ordinarily light on his feet, the jaunty bounce in his step slowed to a lumbering slog as if life was hurting him. I quietly wondered what became of the energetic young man with a natural, cherubic smile. He seemed to withdraw into himself. Perhaps it was the safest place for him.

Anil was born in India, and as he described it to me, it was a traditional and somewhat rigorous upbringing. In his village, it was not unusual for young children, especially boys under the age of ten, to contribute to family life by working in the fields. It was a way of preparing young men to be the eventual leaders of the extended family unit. It was a typical patriarchal household where the men made most decisions while the women were responsible for domestic duties.

Anil asked me if he could dine with his wife at the hotel's restaurant. He said it was an important evening for him, and he insisted I meet his young bride. The evening appeared to be uneventful. The following day he thanked me, but not before his defenses crumbled while emotions flowed freely. The reason for his recent odd behavior became more apparent. He explained to me through tears that the previous evening was a reconciliation dinner for him and his wife, or it was at least a final attempt. Still, it wasn't enough. Upon returning home, she reaffirmed her desire for a divorce. They failed to bridge the cultural divide and married for only a short time; he was facing a painful and shameful separation.

Anil described the humiliation and embarrassment that accompanies divorce in the Hindu religion. Although she was American, the wife of a Hindu man is supposed to understand her place by honoring her husband under almost all circumstances. She is expected to take a subordinate role and respect her decision to marry into a respectable Indian family. In a culture where maintaining honor was of utmost importance, his family may shame him should she initiate divorce proceedings. His family would surely question why he was unable to control his wife and why he couldn't keep his house in order.

Then he disappeared. He stopped coming to work, and all attempts to reach him were unsuccessful. A week went by, and then two. It didn't occur to me or anyone else to call the authorities. He was a grown man, and adults are free to move about as they wish. We didn't know of any family members he had until a call came in one night to Patrick, his friend, and coworker. Patrick found me that evening and said, "It's over. He's dead." A proud and stout man of determined bearing, he immediately turned on his heels to save himself the embarrassment of an uninhibited display of emotion. I knew immediately of whom he was speaking. I didn't have to ask.

I wept for Anil and at the unexpected loss of a precious and hopeful life taken too soon. I felt a wave of enormous guilt since I was unable to help him more than I did. I believed that somehow I failed him by not recognizing all the signs of the burden he was carrying. I assumed he was distraught over the disintegration of his marriage. But I was unable to know that his powerlessness to keep the union whole sent him hurtling into the vortex of a deep and unrelenting depression. He banked all his happiness on the marriage, saving little else.

Just before the funeral, they displayed his body in an open casket. A white surgical bandage wrapped the upper portion of his head entirely. Following the service, I spoke with his grief-stricken wife. She thanked me for being his friend. As painful as it must have been for her, I had to know what became of him. Knowing the details of his passing was not just macabre curiosity. In the wake of sudden and tragic death, we often want to feel a greater sense of identity and compassion with those most affected. So my queries were an attempt to help increase the level of my empathy for her and him.

She explained that she left him shortly after their dinner at the hotel. She flew to Seattle to seek solace within the warm embrace of family and old friends. It was there where she found Anil—parked in front of her hotel with a bullet ripped through his brain. By his side were a revolver and a one-way flight receipt. He was twenty-six years old.

The bandage was there to spare his family from the reality of what he did to himself. Even in death, his wife was shielding him, protecting his legacy from speculation and further moral erosion of his character. By trying to conceal the real cause of his death, she was reconfiguring his value set for the benefit of his remaining family. It was better they believe he suffered a traumatic accident. Shame is a powerful motivator.

The six-hour plane ride provided Anil time alone to ponder his self-induced demise. I wondered about the places his tormented mind must have taken him while on the long journey. What hellish forces occupied his thoughts and steeled his destructive resolve to continue with the plan? Given the length of the flight, I concluded that his depraved determination must have extended preparations to the following day. With restless sleep providing no respite or a change in his state of mind, he proceeded to secure a vehicle. He then had to locate and purchase a weapon. He succeeded in reducing his life choices to an ordinary calculation, a lethal window of opportunity—six hours, and a day.

My mind questioned if it was an act of deliberation, a carefully choreographed sequence of his final moments on earth. Indeed, he exercised a generous amount of thoughtful planning. Or was he in the throes of disengagement from rational consciousness so profound that his thought processes detached and fled to a place where he failed to recognize himself, resulting in a complete breakdown of identity?

Anil's life didn't end with a single gunshot. It ended when he succumbed to the isolator of depression. His wife explained that as they tried to become more progressively American, he struggled with his traditionalist family being less supportive of their choices. Not able to fight battles on multiple fronts—her feelings, his family, and the shame he felt—he turned inward, a self-quarantine with pain as a constant companion. With his regressed mind seeking safety, his psyche formed a protective shell to shield him from what it couldn't control. It was the same wall that prevented him from sharing his pain.

He became a victim of a clash of values in a society that doesn't encourage its men to display emotional weakness. The result is a culturally induced resistance, a collective negative opinion about the relative value of mental health services, despite the disproportionate death rate of young Indian males resulting from poor relationships and excessive expectations. Members of a society will not subscribe to the need for such services if they don't feel those services are required.

Over the years, I thought about what became of his young wife and the results of a spousal suicide. There are always at least two parties to the ultimate act of self-destruction. The surviving spouse is left with visions that the person they loved committed an unconditional act of selfishness, or perhaps worse, an act of depraved retribution, a final assault on her, and those left behind.

Developing a narrative that made sense must have been an enormous burden as she faced a bewildering latitude of emotions following his demise—shame, isolation, guilt, anger, confusion, shock. She also contended with the rituals of his culture, which may have had limitations on the grieving process. That is victimhood turned upside down. It remains one of the rare occurrences when the victim feels like a perpetrator as they replay the images of their loved one's final moments to understand better what they never saw coming.

I didn't remain in contact with her. Patrick descended into alcoholism, never to be heard from again. We all had to go back to the business of living. My final remembrance of her was of a solitary figure, alone in her grief. She was so young to have been burdened by the complicated heartbreak and the anguish of many unanswered questions.

We all leave a legacy when we depart this earth. What he left behind was the unfulfilled promise of his life, a life she shared. One perhaps forever be defined by nothing more than an unforgiving measure of time.

Six hours, and a day.

Chapter 13

KEVIN AND THE MAN-KING

"We live in capitalism, its power seems inescapable—but then, so did the divine right of kings. Any human power can be resisted and changed by human beings. Resistance and change often begin in art. Very often in our art, the art of words." — *Ursula K. Le Guin*

A MAN-KING IS UNREHABILITATED AND UNHEALED; he displays the classic signs of malignant narcissism with a grandiose sense of self-importance. Unapologetically arrogant and at the epicenter of his universe, he makes himself the nucleus of everyone else's world. His relationships with coworkers are exploitive and cruel, designed to elevate his status at the diminished esteem of others.

A humble leader recognizes that they don't have all the answers. They want to share good ideas and team success. They welcome feedback, creativity, and constructive criticism. A Man-King however, sets himself up as a deity, all-knowing and all-powerful. Like oxygen to a fire, he continuously fuels his neuroses by relentlessly seeking opportunities to control and strengthen his house of psychological pain.

Any self-endowed king of the castle must live up to his self-proclaimed superiority. Doing any less means failure, and barbarians rarely admit to failure. The flawed notions of grandeur that reside in their psyche must be proven and reinforced in the real world and with real people. Working people are the tools or the means to a Man-King's nefarious end, which is his never-ending quest for affirmation. For his employees, it is a debilitating and self-perpetuating cycle of anxiety-inducing drama. It is exhausting for them to try to live up to expectations that usually are unclear as they seek to out-maneuver their Man-King's unpredictability.

Kevin was a seasoned and successful hotel sales executive. While on a friendly visit and property tour with Kevin, he introduced me to the Man-King. Before the meeting, as a favor to Kevin, I arranged a golf round for Man-King and his friends at one of my company's golf courses. Although I was a stranger to him, I bought a sleeve of golf balls for him and his friends as a welcome gift. It was one of those things we do for one another as senior hospitality professionals, the gesture more significant than the value of the offering. I found it oddly inappropriate that he didn't acknowledge that I extended the margins of good will.

At first encounter, he was a man entirely comfortable wearing power and arrogance on his sleeve. He had a deep, resonating voice and a sideways half-smile as if part of his mouth was bothered by the effort. While chatting with him, he curiously leveled a playful but awkwardly misplaced insult at Kevin. When I asked Kevin if his boss was usually so complacent with strangers, all he could do was scratch his head and wonder the same. But my antenna went up immediately. As an observer of people, I thought his tight-lipped smirk revealed a smugness, a boastful self-satisfaction he had no intention of concealing. However, my brief encounter with him was just an omen of worse things to come.

Kevin was still new to his job and hadn't yet experienced the full-force, workplace brutality of which Man-King was capable. Shortly after, I began receiving alarming texts from Kevin. The messages barely hid his disbelief as he described recent encounters with Man-King, who was growing increasingly more comfortable in his role as a provocateur. The barbs that began as verbal jousting became more personal and more stinging. It is predictable behavior from workplace bullies. They take time to size up their prey and evaluate soft targets. Careful at first to stick their toe in the water, they gauge a victim's reaction for clues for how much they can get away with.

That is what Man-King was doing during my first meeting with him. Through me, he was squaring up his opportunity to make Kevin one of his future objects of ridicule. Still, what began as playful sparring was morphing into something much more sinister. He floated his trial balloons with Kevin and other intended victims. Eventually, he learned what frontiers he was comfortable crossing. His intensity and boldness were escalating, and those outside of his circle were the most vulnerable.

It is essential, however, to distinguish "the circle." Even a dictator can't subsist and thrive without a support system—a buffer of accomplices and enablers. The members of the circle do not necessarily behave with a nefarious star-chamber aura of superiority. If asked, none of the inhabitants of Man-King's intimate circle would admit to being part of an inner sanctum. In a more precise sense, they would be correct. With most of these situations, the participants are ordinary employees who have found a way to navigate and survive the boss's quirks, thus landing them in good grace.

In some cases, the members of the circle are conspiratorial followers bound by a shared purpose. In the environment rife with negativity, paranoia, suspicion, and raging ego, they jockey for approval. No one at its hostile core wants to be the one not to do well. So the circle is one of loose psychological assembly. But it also places its members on a slippery slope. To remain safe, the members must appear to support the barbarian while maintaining cordial relations with colleagues in different divisions. Still, they sold their souls to the devil in exchange for unspoken immunities and protections unavailable to Kevin and others. Nevertheless, Man-King successfully manipulated selected associates to sow the seeds of perpetual mistrust, placing a schism between them and the rest of the team members.

Each day presented a new opportunity for Man-King. The venue to do his worst was the DBB, the daily business briefing, which was an informal meeting of senior managers at the top of the morning to discuss the day's business at hand. But the venue makes the opportunity. The DBB was the stage, and Man-King was the lead performer, the star of his show.

Since a performer without an audience is someone talking to himself, Man-King made the moment, and he wrote his script to engage in public character assassination. His intended victims could be anyone among the captive onlookers. It was a brilliant setup, built to be ruthlessly effective at humiliating unsuspecting dupes. For Man-King, the thrill of the hunt was as exciting as the kill. What better way to satisfy a craven, hungry beast than by cornering his unsuspecting quarry in a ready-made ambush?

One day, Man-King decided to shame Kevin at the DBB publicly. He lasered in on Kevin's attire by asking him where he purchased his suits. He asked Kevin if he shopped for his clothing at Walmart. Stunned by the irrelevant line of questioning, Kevin responded that it didn't matter where he bought his apparel. Nevertheless, he replied that his suits were custom-tailored and expensive. Kevin's response only provided more ammunition for Man-King, who then asked Kevin if he kept cute little red shoes under his desk.

The barbarian had ensnared Kevin in a classic frame-up by false supposition, forcing him to publicly disprove a fallacy. The barely hidden implication was if Kevin did buy his suits at Walmart, there would be shame, but if he didn't, he must be gay. Kevin continued to ask about the relevance of his clothing in a meeting meant to discuss the business of the day. But Man-King was undeterred. Not content to give up his prey, he continued pricking Kevin for the remainder of the day with personal jabs about his attire. For Man-King, the written rules safeguarding employees from harassment were nothing more than inconvenient scribblings to make paper planes.

Outrageously enough, but not content to settle for denigrating Kevin's choice of suits, Man-King transitioned seamlessly and effortlessly to his weight. Kevin's sales team decided to form a ketogenic diet club. By creating a volunteer association, the participants could share exercise tips, ideas, recipes, stories of encouragement, and rally each other to live healthier lifestyles. The team members set goals and staged regular weigh-ins.

One weigh-in day also happened to be Kevin's birthday, a festive opportunity for everyone except Man-King. Never one to partake in such triteness, Man-King was not in a celebratory mood. Nevertheless, he summoned the enthusiasm to inform Kevin to go weigh in because he "above all people needed to lose a few pounds." Naturally, Man-King chose to hurl the insult in front of an audience for maximum impact.

I informed Kevin that this behavior crossed a line from garden-variety idiocy and into the realm of sexual harassment. When I asked how this conduct wasn't a matter for the human resources office, Kevin replied that human resources did not engage in employee advocacy. Their limited role was to expedite benefits and record events relating to employee discipline. That explained Man-King's shocking audacity. The human resources director was firmly under Man-King's control, placing him in a position of perfectly consolidated power. So for the distressed or bullied employee, there wasn't a safety net or a sheltered place to land.

After a while, and no longer to anyone's profound disbelief, Man-King seamlessly shifted tactics to keep everyone off-balance by proclaiming that his entire management staff was unprofessional and incompetent. It was a deliberate attempt to telegraph his totalitarian desire to eventually purge the ranks of anyone in disagreement with him. It was his graceless way of laying the groundwork for a series of terminations for cause, thus precluding the need to pay for severance or unemployment insurance compensation.

His constant saber-rattling and ostentatious display of power shifted reasonable minds from production to basic survival. Entirely contrary to conventional hospitality thinking, Man-King shamelessly claimed the hotel was about him and not his paying guests. He doubled down on his conceit by demanding his staff refuse to perform the services required by their clients and hotel guests without first doing what was acceptable to him.

Not content with the abuse he regularly rained down on his people, Man-King summoned his entire staff to the DBB. It was here where he made his most logic-defying decree. From a throne not big enough to hold him, he declared Florida was a right-to-work state and he could fire anyone at will and whenever he pleased. He announced that firings would begin if sales did not double in the next year. He further revealed that if someone dared speak up in retaliation to anyone outside the hotel, he would blacklist the employee to prevent them from obtaining future work in the city. To no one's surprise, Man-King succeeded in creating an environment of open warfare—on the same people he needed for his very survival.

Again, my mind went to the role of the hotel's human resources office. The director was present in the room at the time. When questioned how she could permit such blatant abuse of authority, she fecklessly explained her role was only to record the proceedings. The relationship between the boss and human resources is usually a symbiotic one. Unfortunately, she was fearful of losing her job, as well. It was pure skullduggery, and I scrolled the recesses of my mind to try and remember when I saw or heard of such evil in the workplace. I couldn't.

Tyrannically primed for battle and highly intelligent, Man-King could slay with a thousand small cuts, making daily existence a living hell for his staff. Still, his latest assertion signaled an escalation of cruelty. Denigrating behavior becomes progressively more erratic when it is unchecked. Without self-awareness, the swollen ego seeks a higher threshold of stimulation to satisfy its desire for dominance. Each incremental step of barbarity becomes a new normal as its boundary of acceptance or apathy by others moves proportionally.

Man-King had ingeniously, but not subtly, manipulated reasonable people to reassess and realign their margins of social tolerance. Besieged employees often seek psychological safety when potential economic ruin is the alternative. By shifting their level of approval, they remain temporarily out of harm's way, relieved that the suffering of others hasn't touched them.

Against this landscape, Kevin felt compelled to do something he never believed he would do. He was about to contract a $25,000 conference for the hotel, which would have paid him a handsome commission. Kevin knew he wouldn't be in his present job long enough to help expedite the conference when it eventually happened. So he made an excuse and quietly shifted the contract to a competing hotel. Cautiously, he and his team began to engage in sabotage—the byproduct of endless assaults on their value systems.

Kevin and his associates described a feeling of the extreme devaluation of their self-worth, like living in an abusive relationship. They knew they had to leave their employment, but life's circumstances aren't always in alignment with the necessity for a sudden departure from one's livelihood. Still, Man-King succeeded in reducing them to soldiers clustered in a kill zone, no one wanting to die alone. All they could do was watch each other's backs and hope for relief to come from somewhere or someone.

Eventually, Kevin and others resigned their positions. Once, they were proud industry professionals with substantial credentials. Battle-weary, and weakened by stress-related fatigue, they decided they'd endured too many sleepless nights. But in the end, it was Man-King who leveled a final assault. He kept a long stick in his office with the painted names of all the associates who left him, betrayed him. Like cutting a notch in his gun, it was a tool to relive the thrill of his kills. It is a characteristic of sadists to keep trophies memorializing their experiences, the same way people bring home souvenirs from a vacation. The stick was Man-King's aberrant way of extending the fantasy of his victories, rolling in the dirt of the memory of those who abandoned him, and forever burnishing their tarnished names in his mind.

Chapter 14

HENRY AND THE HIGH PRICE OF PRODIGY

"Everybody detests an old head on young shoulders."
— Unknown

THEY WERE DESCRIBED to me as the chosen few, and they formed a new company from a loose assembly of senior-level industry executives with a wealthy benefactor. Henry, barely out of his twenties, was a member of the company and recently promoted from the ranks. Of course, such promotions can be positive.

Many companies elevate senior leaders almost exclusively from within to stay ahead of the learning curve. These opportunities can also backfire if the candidate is too underdeveloped to assume the responsibility of top-level leadership, which includes managing other senior leaders. Henry was competent and skilled within his confined space. But his rapid ascent to the throne reinforces that a baseball team's slow-footed first baseman who hits thirty home runs isn't always the best player on the field.

There may have been more deserving and experienced candidates—business-savvy men and women who spent years in the field, making senior decisions, and managing hundreds of real-life situations. Perhaps the promotion was an easy decision to make. Although for the teams on the ground, it was their hope and anticipation that Henry would at least recognize his lofty status with humility by building trust slowly; to learn and observe, knowing he was among more senior leaders.

Taking nothing away from promoting the devil you know and so on, it is merely a cop-out to elevate the one familiar to you because it involves less possible grief down the road. Before they know it, the recently promoted young manager is in a role where they have glaring industry knowledge gaps. Still, the expectation is that they lead older workers with years or decades of quantifiable successes. Unless they take the opportunity to develop the necessary interpersonal skills such as building trust, the inevitable outcome is hostility and resentment.

I don't present this chapter to theorize about our associates born between 1980 and 1996. There is a substantial amount of published information and misinformation about this group. I have read too many unflattering portraits of these industrious workers. They are usually sweeping, knee-jerk generalizations loosely positioned as indisputable facts. While such unfortunate characterizations provide entertaining reading, the experience of leaders who manage younger colleagues is subjective.

There are always difficult employees and difficult people. These are our management challenges, and they come in all shapes, sizes, and age groups. The younger generation has always provided good-old-days nostalgic fodder for those who preceded them. The newer cohort of employees doesn't hold the monopoly on entitlement, insolence, and insubordination. In twenty-five years battling militant unions, my most significant challenges were from those who believed they had lived long enough to learn all the tricks of psychological warfare. Entitlement doesn't discriminate by age.

Undoubtedly, this entrepreneurially minded age group has entered the workforce with stunning business potential. From a sociocultural perspective, these associates believe they can accomplish more with less. As a result, they are, at times, pejoratively and unfairly maligned as representatives of an uninformed generation.

Most of us spend forty-five-to-fifty years working, toiling to help make someone else wealthy. Our younger team members see a different path. They see a trail that has already been blazed by the rising tide of brilliant, young, tech-minded entrepreneurs. However, for those not fortunate enough to work for themselves, they still reside in offices across the land, and many carry the same restless appetite for immediate gratification.

This group is associated with an intense desire to experience a meteoric rise to the top—an attempt to escape the grind of the dues-paying culture of their parents and grandparents. However, there is consequential damage that accompanies such lofty ambition. No doubt, there are legions of intelligent, savvy, future stars. But the operative word is "future."

Henry found out there is no replacement for the deftness and skill that experience provides. That would be knowing how to solve problems by leveraging cross-functional relationships and developing the competencies which enable young managers to work effectively in a team environment built on a diverse platform of people with various abilities.

Those in the trenches are sensitized to the leader who swoops in to save the day, or to criticize from afar. It doesn't take a specialized talent to find fault when you believe your role is to identify the lint in the corner of the room, and Henry arrogantly played the part of the perfectionist imposter. Eager to make his mark, he was quick to issue decrees based on his limited exposure to existing processes—methods implemented previously to reduce unnecessary time and motion. Nevertheless, Henry, always ready with a cliché, decried that such practices were the result of lazy staff members accustomed to convenient shortcutting. Too green to the art of constructive discontent, he didn't care to ask if the procedures he was anxious to replace were the tools of survival that managers before him deemed necessary.

Sometimes inexperienced leaders with a shiny new crown use perfectionism as a ploy to mask insecurity or deflect from their lack of experience. They use carefully timed opportunities to dazzle and impress or express dominion over longer-tenured employees—associates who the barbarian believes suffer from a deficiency of enlightened thinking. However, Henry didn't know he was hiding what he didn't know, and vulnerability wasn't a skill he acknowledged or chose to use.

In the article, *The Young and the Clueless*, published in the *Harvard Business Review*, the author forewarned a future when bosses would elevate underlings too quickly for fear of losing their young talent to a competitor. In the process, the newly minted bosses fall victim to their ambition and lack of generalship. Their accomplishments loom large, but those successes, although admirable, do not address the foundational requirements, the building blocks to be able to negotiate with, and to persuade peers and subordinates when necessary, or to regulate emotions in a period of crisis.[xiii]

The newly promoted young leader soon learns a proportional relationship exists between the size of their new leather chair and the capabilities others expect them to have. These aren't skills found in a textbook. In many cases, the boss who advances too soon, with qualifications based on a specific skill, doesn't know how they are perceived. Understanding people and studying human behavior is a lifelong endeavor and a lesson in knowing the value of social capital. It is only with time that we know what buttons to push for whom and when.

As the new young boss, like Henry, finds out, and sometimes too late, the need for more considerable soft skills often runs in a parallel line with a fancier job title. The *Harvard Business Review* article said that it is one thing to understand the importance of relationships at an intellectual level and to learn techniques like active listening and processing employee complaints. However, it is another matter to fully understand interpersonal skills such as patience, positive engagement, openness, empathy, and the willingness to admit failure. The development of soft skills involves a fundamental shift in self-awareness requiring practice.

The results of several recent high-profile cases provide credible testimony to the *Harvard Business Review* article's assertions. Away, Uber, WeWork, the Dallas Mavericks, and countless other companies have had young leaders come under fire, resulting in quantum changes in top-level leadership. In all the cases, the common threads were accusations of harassment, unjust terminations, shady dealings, and unfair or inhumane working conditions. Despite performance, talent, and drive, there is still a vast dissimilarity between excelling at specific aptitudes and having the ability to lead.

The skilled adults around Henry only endured so much from him, as they would any young leader trying to flex their muscles. Accomplished senior professionals with the benefit of perspective see through, knowing what the young barbarian doesn't know. Knowledgeable and respected team members are practitioners of calm. They know the weight of the crown. They see that a crown placed on the wrong head has thorns. Experienced workers know with whom they want to be in the trenches when a firefight starts. And no one wants to be in the foxhole with a liability—a leader they do not believe is authentic and one whose self-interests precede theirs.

Henry also struggled with messaging. Oblivious to his mangled syntax, he nevertheless fancied himself a great orator, standing before worshippers while delivering keynote speeches of great importance. However, learning to speak eloquently and clearly before a mixed group of spectators takes practice and self-confidence. If the message a barbarian delivers routinely contains the stilted language of intimidation, he or she will most likely strain to provide nuanced and effective communication to a broader audience where tones of gradation are as significant as the message itself.

It wasn't an unusual occurrence for the eyes in the room to roll and drift once Henry stood to convey, at least what he believed, was rousing dialogue—language which was supposed to create positive momentum and to enlighten. Unfortunately, credibility and trust are the casualties of emotionally dishonest communication.

In most cases of the hostile environment created by the inexperienced leader, options are limited. It is sometimes possible to take a grievance up the ladder of command. But doing so assumes there is someone up the chain who will listen. The second option is to meet the offender where they stand; the best defense is a strategically crafted offense. There is a portion of respect to be gained by keeping one's ground. For good measure, it helps to remind the young bully that their status outstrips their ability. However, only someone confident, self-assured, and practiced at decisive confrontation can deliver the message. One must also be careful of retaliation. Although companies have strict no-retaliation policies, there are crafty methods to circumvent such systems.

The third option is to wait for an opportunity to leave on one's terms. And at least, in this case, many did. After the company tried to cut its way to profitability by decimating senior leadership ranks, Henry had to go back into the field to pick up the pieces. It wasn't long before the remaining middle managers also departed. The fourth possible scenario is to wait for the barbarian to leave the company. Henry eventually did, essentially throwing in the towel after surveying the depth of the operational damage done by the ill-advised purge of the leadership ranks and its resulting attrition.

They handed Henry a crown. But a heavy crown can break a neck.

Chapter 15

DREAM CHASER, P.F.C.

"All men dream: but not equally. Those who dream by night in the dusty recesses of their minds wake up in the day to find it was vanity, but the dreamers of the day are dangerous men, for they may act their dreams with open eyes, to make it possible." — T.E.Lawrence

WE KNOW THE dreamer. The mail clerk saves to buy his first home, the waitress who wants to be a movie star, and the busboy working to open a small restaurant because he learned it is possible. It is the dreamer who keeps the flame of hope alive because that is what it means to live in a free society. We work to enrich life, to validate our existence. The dreamers tell us that anything and everything is possible. It is the dreamer who captures the essence of the American Dream, a thoroughly American experience.

"It is the notion of upward mobility, the idea that one can, through dedication and with a can-do spirit, climb the ladder of success and reach a higher social and economic position. For many in both the working class and the middle class, upward mobility has served as the heart and soul of the American Dream, the prospect of betterment, and to improve one's lot for oneself and one's children."[xiv]

Perhaps dreams are only a product of our imagination. Nevertheless, they remain deeply woven into the fabric of our working lives. No other concept has as much influence on our lives, and there isn't an alternative idea that leaves us with as much elation, sorrow, joy, or dissatisfaction.

Dreams—we chase them, although they are always a step ahead. We reach but rarely do we grasp them. Like the drug or bottle that some can't get enough of, we pursue them. Or maybe they are like the tantalizing seductiveness of a deeply intoxicating relationship, the kind that brushes against a different dimension, rearranges consciousness, and alters our rational thoughts.

Since dreams are a self-authorizing concept, we can put them away for another day, and then another. But they are relentless. They are patient as they wait for us to lose our breath, the deep sighs a constant reminder of loss—loss of opportunity, identity, and loss of life's meaning.

They thrive in the disorder of personal confusion, fear, and indecision. Dreams are intelligent, knowing soon enough, we run out of time, life's most precious commodity. Sometimes we feel we are too late and too old to chase a new dream, but not too young to be haunted by them. And that is the thing about dreams. We can't take them with us. But there they are, enduring, tolerant, and ruthless, daring us to try to meet them where they stand.

Those stubborn dreams...

The one thing he wanted more than anything was to be a military officer. He was the second child born to first-generation immigrants, but with a ten-year separation between his older brother and himself, he might have been an only child. Growing up in the aftermath of World War I and shaped by the Great Depression's demanding realities, he learned the necessities of self-reliance and accountability—absolute prerequisites for effective leadership at a young age. While his older brother yearned to heal others in the pristine quarters of hospital hallways, he longed to lead men in the fog of battle.

At sixteen, he applied for officer candidate school. He falsified his age by saying he was eighteen, and they expelled him before he started. When he was old enough to reapply, they told him his eyesight was too weak. Undeterred, and so fierce was his desire to serve and sacrifice, he enlisted in the regular army on February 10, 1941.

Military leaders tend to be autonomous and with an elevated desire for control. However, for him, it was never about the power, the prestige, or the accolades which may have followed. It was about a conscious choice and deeply ingrained desire to serve first, to inspire, and to be where the action was. He was built for stress, always willing to show up to give more than he ever received. It was a recurring theme through the remainder of his life.

He joined as a rank private, and along the way, he was conscientious enough to rise to the sergeant's rank, at least until he fell asleep on watch and lost his stripes. He always did like his catnaps. He was in Belgium in the spring of 1945. Shortly after that, he was in Germany training for an amphibious assault on mainland Japan. Perhaps by God's grace or good fortune, he narrowly missed the Battle of the Bulge, and he later escaped certain death when the events of Hiroshima and Nagasaki meant he could finally come home in the fall of that year.

He departed as a boy and returned as a man. Like so many, he was thrust into adulthood, wandering about without vision or a clearly defined path. He settled into a mundane existence many veterans faced following the great war. In a way, it was a tragic story that played out in countless homes across the landscape. He searched and failed at many things. He tried to emulate his older brother, the successful medical doctor, living and playing at the country club. Just like his brother, he applied for admission to Georgetown University's School For The Study of Diplomacy.

I imagine how his eyes must have beamed reading his letter of acceptance. As a youngster, I rarely saw that sparkle. But on that day and for a brief, shining moment, he must have felt exultant. He may have even smiled broadly, although a smile never came naturally to him. As a child, the face I knew was worn by discontent, with frown lines deeply ingrained by muscle memory. What may have passed for a fleeting smile was stiff and awkward since he was unaccustomed to expressing unbridled joy.

Wanting to make up for lost time, he tried to do too much, too soon, and he failed out of the prestigious school, Georgetown. Another dream shattered. He finished his education at night school and dutifully got married. After that, life for him became a never-ending grind of multiple jobs, surviving but never thriving while living a minimalist existence to provide the basic requirements for a growing family.

He was an unremarkable man, yet he was everyman. He failed but never defined himself by loss. He was too dutiful, too proud, and too stubborn not to fight again and again. His greatest pleasure, perhaps the one thing that would have alighted his sad eyes, was seeing me go to West Point. Although at age eighteen, I was having none of it.

I didn't know him growing up. I never saw him, except on Sundays. The joke with the punchline of the man walking miles to work, uphill both ways? When our family car broke down, we didn't have a car. Still, he had highly protective instincts, and as tireless as he was, he walked to his second job. It was part-time evening work collecting tolls on the bridge. He walked there both ways to support a family with a wife and three small toddler boys in the 1960s. And yes, it was four miles each way. He later sold suits at E.J. Korvettes, an old neighborhood version of Sears or Kohl's. It was another second job. Or maybe a third job. I don't remember. He loved his suits, but he was no salesperson.

He often dreamed of a better life. He imagined aloud, but without the bluster or the swaggering promise of great things to come. He was too uncomfortable in his skin to ever call attention to himself. His dreams were big. Although without a plan, they lacked the strength of conviction. Goals without a higher purpose or the skills to fulfill those hazy dreams are just wishes. Like so many, he was more fearful of the unknown than he was of the banality of his existence, one he tragically learned to live with, and one I never heard him protest. With his disillusionment successfully internalized, the irony wasn't lost on me that the life he so desperately wanted, one of logistical maneuvering, duty, and obligation, was precisely the life he had. It was just never on his terms.

I remember when he finally retired. He didn't play golf or fish or have a hobby to fill his time, and I wondered what he would do with himself since he was always a restless one. He began to outlive his intimate group of family and friends, and I flippantly asked him if he was waiting to die. He didn't need or want a hobby. He was content to take a long and well-earned reprieve from a life he had spent providing for others before taking care of himself.

As I learned to know him better in retirement, I realized those deep breaths were, sadly, the exhalations of a man who learned to live with disappointment. He didn't chase his dreams as much as they chased him. But with his dreams no longer nipping at his heels, he stopped running. Human nature is remarkably resilient, and he conditioned himself to settle for less from age sixteen until his death almost seventy years later. With his ambitions reduced to primal yearnings for greater appreciation, I believe his diseased heart was only the physical metaphor of a once-promising spirit broken by loss—loss of opportunity, of personal achievement, and desire.

I rarely heard him express his feelings since he was a man of few words. It was never about what he said. It was always about what he did. Modest, generous, self-effacing, and empathetic, he was perhaps ahead of his time, or a result of his time. He lived the life of a servant leader before the term was codified in 1970 by Robert Greenleaf in his essay *The Servant As Leader.* The honesty and integrity that compelled him to want to serve and lead at such a young age never waned. He took it with him.

Through the years, I had an intense desire to make him proud of the work I did. And it wasn't because I felt I must live up to his whimsical expectations of greatness. He would never force me to pray at his altar of personal ambition. I just hoped he knew that his struggle in a lifetime of sacrifice while bringing me up meant something beyond the perfunctory parental obligation.

As he lay dying, it was vital for me to let him know that he didn't fail, that he had done well to teach me to stand tall; to understand how to be counted on; and to be irrepressible, honorable, and ethical. These are the footprints he left behind, the ones I walk in today. It is a debt I can never repay.

Chapter 16

SAVING ANGELS

"Angels come in all sizes and shapes. Yes, sometimes they may even look like truckdrivers." — Unknown

I BELIEVE IN angels. They come by two—the one we see and the one we don't. Angels walk among us. They usually enter our lives by happenstance. Perhaps it was a letter or an unexpected phone call we received—or the uplifting and perfectly timed words of encouragement delivered by someone we barely knew. Maybe they were the only ones who didn't turn their backs when we needed people the most. Still, the otherworldly angel, the one we can't see, comes by design, but not of this earth.

The angels that came to me on an evening many years ago, an evening like any other, didn't know they were saving me. The angel I couldn't see whispered to me and made tracks for me to follow because I didn't see a clear path through the darkness. What I didn't know then was that the invisible angel was always with me—keeping me safe when I could scarcely protect myself. I just had to be where it could touch me, feel me. The angel moved me when it knew I was losing what little self-worth I had left.

An angel came to me again some years later. In a moment of misplaced trust, I cast my lot with a sociopath who sold me a dream. Visions of prosperity can distort reality and make the world seem like a better place. I anguished because his dream became my nightmare. But there in my little daughter's room, I found the place.

The room, decorated in cheerful baby pink, represented a portrait of opposing forces. Inside the small space, the innocence and promise of childhood squared off against the overpowering self-recrimination and disgrace of an unwise adult decision. Mistakes of the past only affected me. However, this latest misjudgment came with substantially more collateral damage—a new home, my baby daughter, and my family.

As small children do, they toss, heave, and pitch whatever might be within arm's reach. Alone, and with nothing to occupy my troubled mind except the fearful contemplations of going back to a desperate place I thought I left behind years ago, I found it. A corner. A place of refuge. It was a perfectly safe space to disappear within myself and allow my firewall to crumble. Until that time, I hid my shame and distress from my wife, friends, and family. I built an illusion, a pillar of emotional strength to shield them from the fear of how desperate I had become. Perhaps the intense fallout from that fateful decision would vanish if I could hide away and pretend to make myself small.

Pulling the crib away to pick up the projectiles, I saw the corner with adjacent and perpendicular walls. I allowed myself to descend, my knees against my chest in an upright fetal position. The walls surrounded me, perfect to hold me up should I decide to fall to one side in a curled posture of submission. Falling over would signal the surrender of whatever fight I had left.

And it was there when it appeared. In my broken state, I heard the patter of little feet coming in my direction. The next sensation I remember was the feeling of small arms wrapped around me, holding me. A tiny hand caressed my shoulder and wiped a tear from my eye. Then the angel, not two years old, quietly whispered, "Daddy…"

In that twinkling in time, I knew I had brushed against the echoes of a world I couldn't explain. And those are the moments we remember all our lives, the moments when there aren't words to narrate our experience—the fleeting flashes of humanity that provide a glimmer of hope when despair is all we see.

But the angels had more work to do. Later, I received an invitation to visit with important people—people who could change things. Nevertheless, months spent surviving the psychological minefield of stress, rejection, and weariness had taken its toll. Little did I know the price I paid for endurance was a sadness so deep that my cognitive mind began to separate and shut parts of itself down in a desperate attempt at self-preservation. I began to see myself outside of my body, looking down at events happening in actual time. It was as if what remained of my overwhelmed rational mind didn't want to suffer what the rest of me was about to do, and it removed itself from reality to avoid further harm.

In this damaged state, I visited with them, the important people. Unable to hide my desperation, I failed with those I met. My injured psyche was unable to manage where my diminished survival mechanisms had taken me. It was a disaster until someone, one of them, said there was another option for me.

After months of denials and discouragement that threatened my dignity, he believed in me when I stopped believing in myself. With an intense, sincere personality and intuition beyond his years, he could see me. In an industry where its culture is driven by people whose positivity and natural enthusiasm routinely extend the borders of natural friendliness, he asked me if I knew how to smile. Taken aback by the question, I lied and said yes, of course, I did. A knowing half-grin creased his lips. I knew then that he still believed.

And that is what angels do. "They are the anchors of awakenings, and they see things, not the way they are, but the way they can be.

They alter perspectives. They change consciousness. They offer a glimmer of hope when confidence and esteem have given way to despair. They are imperfect people sent to learn things about the human condition and guide other beings on earth. They have a deep and abiding confidence in the human spirit to love, endure, and overcome. They are purposeful yet work in the shadows without drawing attention to themselves. They are brave and daring because they go with us to places where there is fear, dread, loneliness, and apprehension."[xv] Angels restore humanity just when someone or something is poised to take it from us. Sometimes they are the recipients of kindness, so they repay benevolence by offering the same for others. Just lost souls saving one another. That is the chain reaction of human compassion.

Angels don't always come when we summon them. They don't happen just by wishing they do. They come when we have learned to excise the restrictive thinking and the shame that binds us. They know to come when we have opened our hearts and minds enough to allow them a place in our lives.

They come when we have prepared the way.

Chapter 17

———— ✺ ————

OUR EMOTIONAL TOOLBOX

"I don't want to be at the mercy of my emotions. I want to use them, to enjoy them, and to dominate them." — *Oscar Wilde*

THE COMPLETE ELIMINATION of disagreeable behavior is a lofty ambition because human nature isn't predictable. We live, learn, and we act. Forecasting the actions and reactions of people with a degree of certainty is like shooting a cue ball into a tight configuration of fifteen billiard balls. The cue shot is the stimulus or the action. The scattering of the pack of balls is the reaction. Like emotions, the balls ricochet and rebound in irregular, unforeseeable patterns with each ball landing in a random space. The balls remain static until another stimulus, a new action, strategically realigns their position for a better eventual outcome. The game is won when a skilled practitioner successfully navigates the nuances and complexities of arbitrary angles and obstacles created by the initial shot.

It is then the capable team leader who competently manages the different effects of an action, or in our analogy, the cue shot. For as long as humans have an ego, there will be behaviors to correct. The leader's objective is not the total elimination of unacceptable behavior, but rather its marginalization. Along the way, effective leaders learn what to do because they have seen what not to do.

Pattern detection is the pivot point for emotionally and socially intelligent people who seek to understand and resolve conflicts that stand in the way of the natural ebb and flow of successful business interactions. The Stealth Warrior, William, Man-King, and the Mistress of the Scorched Earth, among others, are anecdotal examples of anti-modeling. By recognizing the consequences from the expression of their destructive behaviors, we know which character traits to avoid.

We can trace the objectionable behavior of our chapter subjects back to a failure to identify with one or more of the five values described below. These skills serve as the components of our wellness toolkit.

#1. FEEL. THINK. REACT.

Most of the impactful decisions we make in our lives do not begin with a thought, but with a feeling. Reflect on an occasion when you made a significant purchase or jumped into a pristine lake from a high perch or spoke in public for the first time. Before you acted, a part of your brain processed a feeling. A thought came a second later, and before you took measurable action.

The feelings and emotions we have come from our unconscious brain. They develop in the early stages of life. They are formed in part by DNA, our upbringing, education, life experiences, and circumstances, as well as the evolutionary development of behaviors and physiological mechanisms many years in the making. It is our unique ability to feel, which makes us truly human. Because we can feel for ourselves, we know we feel for others.

That is what Dr. Jay Lombard refers to in his seminal book *The*

Mind of God: Neuroscience, Faith, And A Search for The Soul, as the work of mirror neurons. These are transmitters in the brain that connect our shared experiences. If we watch someone place their hand on a hot flame, we wince for them, producing similar, but different, sensations of pain. It is as if our brain's neurons are reflecting someone else's to create a shared reaction. Therefore, these neurons are not only reflective, but also interpretive. They help us decode the meaning of our behavior to point to something beyond ourselves.[xvi]

When we integrate our natural emotions with our rational brain to shape action and form a more in-depth interpretation of others' needs, we have discovered the "Aha!" moment, the cornerstone of compassionate human relations. It is a circuitry process representing the elevation of affective empathy to form cognitive empathy, or the ability to reflexively assimilate gut instincts with our thinking brain to know a walk in someone else's shoes. We can, thereby, develop a greater sense of identity with what others are experiencing. Without the capacity to feel, the cognitive brain is not called upon to qualify our emotions or to provide restrictions for them, resulting in actions or reactions which are either inappropriate, or improper.

When we engage with intent to serve others, it is an act that begins with a single feeling, delivered by those with the innate capacity to please, to empathize, and to understand. People with the natural aptitude to please believe in the service advocacy model, which is the foundation for hospitality, and we can't believe in what we don't feel.

When we fully leverage our ability to feel, we transcend what is immediately apparent. The desire to serve—to advocate, engage, anticipate needs, to expand the latitude of generosity—begins with our ability to feel, which is to understand emotions and intent. Once we generate a feeling, we then employ our thinking brain to size it up. And finally, we react appropriately, which produces a positive outcome for both the beneficiary of service and for its provider.

Feel, think, react. Time and again.

#2. MANAGE YOUR MAGNIFICENT EGO, OR HOW TO PUT YOUR WEAPONS DOWN.

During the mid-1970s, there was a commercial for Equitable Life Insurance with a tag line, "There's nobody else exactly like you." Indeed, the crowning glory of human beings is we have a unique identifier, making us unlike anyone else. That identifier is the ego. It is the thinking, feeling, and willing "I" of a person that distinguishes them from all other living creatures.

During this lengthy process, I have learned that the ego, our proprietary blueprint, has been telling us stories. It has shown us how to think, what to believe, and how we should manage the forces of life. Therefore, our natural inclination is to embrace our reality—a reality framed by our experiences and only by what we see and hear. Consequently, the ego is a self-limiting restrictor of values shaping our personality. When not adequately filtered, we form emotional connections to our opinions, which prevent us from examining or embracing other points of view.

When inevitable conflict occurs, the hyper-aroused ego seeks comfort and goes outside of itself to find it. It looks for it in associates, coworkers, bosses, friends, parents, partners, etc. It wreaks havoc along the way by overreacting to anger, insecurity, stress, and jealousy. At the same time, it basks in the self-inured embrace and learned helplessness of perpetual victimhood.

That is the irony of the runaway ego. In these situations, unchecked emotion is a puppet master that controls the self-reflection process, making it almost impossible to make the necessary and desperately needed changes to an already misguided value system. It is not coincidental that most conflict in the workplace is simply a clash, the mismanagement of egos in self-preservation mode. In a dispute, we battle to protect our righteous self, and we go to great lengths to defend our stories.

The same ego preservation dynamic plays out in homes across the landscape. Too many discussions which should center on resolution and the effective management of life's events and challenges descend into struggles of who is right and who is wrong. In these situations, the inflamed ego is an intractable wall of emotional resolution that seeks to reaffirm its territory. It disallows rational thought to be a part of the resolution process, bypassing an opportunity to see the root cause of conflict. In the end, the only recollection anyone has of the argument was that nothing was resolved.

What makes the necessary behavioral adjustment challenging is that we spend years inside of ourselves, reinforcing our belief system with the thoughts we trust have served us well. So the lazy ego, always looking for a safe place, is on cruise control. It doesn't have the horsepower to step outside of itself to seek the unknown because what is unfamiliar can be untidy. It is quite comfortable knowing what it knows since it has settled and learned to live with itself for so long.

Unfortunately, it is here where many of our chapter subjects struggled. We react instinctively and reflexively to the events of life. We are accustomed to believing in the automatic processes, with reactions and habits that have gotten us this far. We all want to think we are intelligent and independent thinkers without having to stop, analyze, and evaluate every impulse. Our reactions to events become so routine that we no longer control them—they are controlling us. But the ego is also a moving target that can change with time if we learn to embrace other people's realities by staying connected to what is essential. If we transcend the limited state of being created by the inflamed ego, we no longer reside at the center of our universe, but in front of it.

We don't accomplish the necessary changes without first acquiring the ability to nurture and to listen. We only develop these skills by letting go of the need to be right. The ego, while telling us how to live, also allows us to command our better selves to evaluate emotions. By leading with modesty and restraint, we can determine what to do with emotions from a position of calmness.

It is then by practicing calmness that we know where our personality and our feelings are taking us. Calmness allows us to appreciate our emotions, creating an opportunity for positive interactions because we know others by knowing ourselves. By having an awareness of possible outcomes in advance, we can shape the nuances of our behavior to achieve desired results.

By mastering the art of calm, we learn to put the aroused ego aside. With the ego tempered and in remission, we open the gates to reflection where the thinking part of our brain can be engaged to help appropriately manage situations. When the powerful ego is uninvolved, the rational mind is free to peel back layers to reveal the core of the matter. We then see interactions in a whole new way, where perceptions of the world are more authentic and real. It is a liberating feeling when the heart is free of the constraints of the inflated and binding sense of self. Only when we successfully let go of arrogance are we able to put our weapons down.

#3. HAVE A FIRM PURPOSE, BUT A FLEXIBLE SYSTEM.

The meteoric rise of e-commerce has forever altered the business landscape. With many competitors selling similar products, the quest for individuality and unique identifiers has become a substantial element of any marketing package. This has compelled companies to focus on the *why* of their business instead of on *what*. The phenomenon has kicked many brick-and-mortar businesses to the curbside and sent the survivors scrambling to understand how to remain relevant.

Similarly, end-users who are driving the rapid change in shopping and buying habits are the same individuals now occupying substantial office space with baby boomers nearing retirement age. They are asking their leaders to be receptive to change and to be more competitive in the marketplace. No longer content to sit on the sidelines, restricted by the few purchasing options once housed under one department store roof, they seek diversity of choice in their spending habits and working lives.

This new opportunity has forced a shift in the business halls of power. The change has forced leaders not to abandon their reason for being, but to re-evaluate methodology and how they get to the end of the race. Leaders now more than ever are charged with building and maintaining a flexible environment through diverse management techniques. The one-size solution to managing people by common denominator is increasingly the practice of a bygone era.

The concept of situational management, as described by the Rutgers School of Business, is an adaptive behavioral style. By having multiple available tools, it is virtually a custom-fit solution for a specific mission or challenge. It is the art of leveraging power instead of using it. Here is where Man-King, and others, missed an opportunity. They were so thoroughly practiced in control that they couldn't see that the most considerable authority was the power they never had to use.

Situational management is the art of strategically revealing personality traits to adapt to the demands of different situations without losing one's identity or surrendering expectations. Our Queen feared that a change in her ruthlessly authoritative style signaled the abandonment of her beliefs and anticipations. Power-hungry people such as she, would never associate management flexibility with a useful tool of stewardship.

Situational management is the ultimate flexible business tool. It telegraphs the desire to manage challenges and circumstances, as opposed to controlling them. Like holding a bird with a broken wing—squeeze lightly, and the bird attempts to fly away; squeeze too tightly, and it may expire. Flexible managers use the gift of acquired knowledge and intuition, or perspective, formulated through the survival of stark realities to teach and coach through trials and workplace troubles.

Our flexible behavioral system must also include as one of its standards the ability to manage perpetual change. Styles, tastes, trends, and desires can change seemingly overnight. Such seismic shifts can have a profound impact on whether we survive or thrive in a fluid environment. The ability to successfully weigh options determines our level of success in a contemporary business setting, which moves at a rapid pace.

The same conscientiousness leaders employ to business metrics must equally apply to parameters of the human condition. Leaders must be able to hold their own among a diverse group of staff members, customers, owners, and shareholders in a world of changing workforce dynamics. They must also navigate emergencies, learn, and assimilate new processes and technologies and manage the stress from workplace factors.

With such a burden, fair or unfair, placed on the modern-day leader, they must skillfully adopt behaviors that lend themselves to greater versatility without lowering expectations of performance.

#4. MANAGE THE POWER GAP.

The difference between the style and expectations of management that I recall from the 1980s through the 1990s compared with today's is a remarkable study in contrast. At its apex, a sharp point defined the pyramid style of the 1980s and prior, where only a few of a company's senior leaders occupied rarified air. It was implicitly understood that there were clear separations, unblurred lines between those at the pinnacle and everyone else. This is a divergence from today's more horizontal model.

We can look to Robert Greenleaf's 1970 essay, *The Servant as Leader*, as the beginning of what we now refer to as the flatter pyramid model. Greenleaf writes, "The servant-leader is a servant first. This person is different from one who is a leader first, perhaps because of the need to assuage an unusual power drive or to acquire material possessions. The leader-first and the servant-first are two extreme types. Between them, there are shadings and blends that are part of the infinite variety of human nature. The difference manifests itself in the care taken by the servant first, to make sure that other people's highest priority needs are being served."[xvii]

Although the smoother plane of the horizontal model doesn't translate well to an organizational chart, at least in its theoretical intent, it is designed to provide greater access to the knowledge base that exists at the very top. It demonstrates the notion that shared knowledge between all layers of the pyramid results in exponential growth and productivity through collaboration, creativity, healthy exchanges of ideas, and shared values.

The horizontal model dispenses with the view that the boss is omnipotent and omniscient. It humanizes and removes them from isolation and connects them to the team in ways unheard of forty years ago. In its purest form, the flatter model reduces the distance between those few at the very top and those in the layers below. It is here where a shared sense of esteem and collaboration originates. When the team does well, it is the result of many contributing voices, each one empowered to invest in the process and to make an impact. Amazing things happen when no one claims the credit of a team's accomplishments.

Managers and leaders like Man-King, William, and the Stealth Warrior, are too self-centered to know their real responsibility is to move people in ways that nurture relationships. They create disparate systems of accountability for self-preservation. With their egos aflame, they don't realize their mission is to breathe life into relationships by placing their team members' interests ahead of theirs. It stands to reason then, that some managers, too absorbed with being served, are psychologically and spiritually unavailable to serve others. Buoyed by the intoxicating feeling of dominion over others, they display little interest in bridging the gap between themselves and their associates.

The manager or leader who fails to serve also miscarries their mandate in other ways. Leadership demands the expression of the true self. People want to be led by someone who they perceive is honest and sincere. They link these character traits to authenticity and transparency. The manager who is too insecure to recognize a mistake or to embrace their fallibility will engage in backpedaling to avoid accountability and miss an opportunity to register the behaviors that define successful leadership.

#5. PRACTICE EMOTIONAL FITNESS.

Successful individuals set their minds to a predetermined pathway, a roadmap of goals and objectives. Singular in resolve, they possess the resilience to overcome obstacles time and again. Peak performers talk about these qualities as absolute prerequisites for achieving success. They use the term of mindset to describe a state of being that transcends desire.

The paradigm of mindset is prevalent in the personal and business coaching world; we are what we think we are, and so on. But what is left when mindset isn't enough? Mindset as a stand-alone construct doesn't provide the necessary skills we need to advance an agenda further. It doesn't account for education, or technical expertise, or a foundation of knowledge born from the calloused realities of life's experiences. Mindset doesn't broaden our perspective or provide the identification of threats and obstacles lurking around the corner. So the concept of mindset is fundamentally self-limiting.

Certainly, grit and perseverance are irreplaceable cornerstones of achievement. They provide the momentum, the wind beneath us to get up a seventh time after falling six times. However, we come full circle when we grasp the next component. It comes after technical expertise, mindset, and commitment. It is the concept of emotional fitness.

Emotional fluency gets to the heart of the matter. It is the capacity to have highly protective instincts that shield our plans from outside distractions. It is the skill of managing emotions and surviving the inevitable stress, which is part and parcel of goal attainment. It sees the consequences of interactions in advance, allowing us to tailor our approach, whether it be negotiating business with suppliers and vendors, managing team members, or persuading a potential investor. It is the foundation for thoughtfulness, and it remains the missing link to successful interpersonal relations. The importance of the elevated mindset that defines determination, as vital as it is, is incomplete without the polished patina of emotional fitness.

The absence of emotional fitness underscores the negative character traits, weaknesses, and actions of many individuals described in this book. It is the insufficiency of psychological health that blazes a muddy trail for the deceitful, disrespectful, unpredictable, and frequently, self-destructive behavior of people, sometimes good people, such as Anil and the Good Chef. Emotional fluency is the indispensable faculty of mind that allows us to overcome raw emotions and not be overtaken by feelings when we can't control reactions.

Emotional fitness by itself is not a tactic or a strategy. It is the result of the careful deployment of calmness, which leads to successful ego management, the holy grail of relationship building.

The person who is mentally fit, and manages their emotions by riding waves of uncertainty, and human frailty, is a dangerous individual.

AFTERTHOUGHTS

Luxury hospitality has been my chosen profession for more than thirty-five years. It can be a stressful world of many choreographed pieces to form a chain of human interaction. The parts operate both independently and in unanimity to create one satisfied consumer at a time. The result of a service interaction is determined only in the context of the individual user experience. The level of satisfaction with the exchange is usually in direct proportion to the level of personal advocacy provided by the service supplier.

It is a business ruled by emotions and sensory experiences. Establishments are judged by what people want and what they smell, hear, taste, or see. It is a stress-filled environment where each transaction creates a perception, either positive or negative. Unquantifiable feelings are the difference between keeping the lights on as a viable business or shuttering the business amidst crushing financial distress.

Hospitality operations are complicated. We sometimes wither under strain to get through the grinder of the day. We have human failures, equipment failures, product failures, and quality failures. Managing expectations under unfavorable conditions can be an exercise in futility. It is impossible to measure how service defects can result in a loss of good will, confidence, prestige, or future opportunity. These are incalculable losses in a purely discretionary environment. The business is fragile that way. Along with the relentless pressure to be on stage, we are evaluated on purely subjective insights.

The business has a cultural problem of intensity, long hours, high burnout, pressure-cooker conditions, and, at times, uncivilized patrons. These factors merge to form incubators of adverse behavior. In many cases, managers, and bad-boy chefs, for example, are just living up to an unflattering stereotype. We do well when teaching processes. But we fall short when we don't explain the nuances of relationship building. The very nature of how we mismanage our greatest asset, our people, is a contributing factor leading to diminished productivity. The industry also has a notoriously high turnover of staff due to the transient nature of its participants. For team leaders, frequent staff turnover means that maintaining consistency is, by far, the most difficult of our core values to follow, and lack of consistency is a precursor to failure.

In the past twenty years, the hospitality industry has created the most jobs. Still, it is a soft underbelly of low-wage jobs, usually without benefits or predictable schedules. These workers often live in the margins while trying to juggle children, daycare, or multiple jobs. They are also inclined to quantify their wages in terms of the next bill to pay. Fifty cents more per hour pays a cell phone bill. Despite the proliferation of the industry with entrepreneurial newcomers jumping over high-entry barriers, the business faces a chronic shortfall of available hands on deck, and there is a fatigue factor when managers are in perpetual training mode.

In many ways, the industry provides the perfect set of circumstances for creating a disproportionate number of workplace barbarians. The relentless drive for relevance, adaptability, market share, pennies-on-the-dollar profit margins, and economic survival is a harbinger of poor behavior. And we do it to ourselves. It is a business that can survive despite those who run it, although there is a difference between surviving and thriving.

This is not to excuse those would-be leaders who should be working for themselves. There are those among us who are ill-equipped to manage people, or processes, or both. Many join the hospitality world for the wrong reasons. These individuals may have a purpose for being where they are, but they lack passion. Without passion for people, they don't have the will to persevere through the many challenges of an unforgiving industry. It is the leader-barbarians who require the most intervention, yet they are generally resistant to behavioral change. They are the ones who have built legacies of mediocrity, fear, and oppression. Still, they value their toxic creations because of their inflamed egos.

Too often, leaders mismanage opportunities because they would rather be right than be smart. They fail to fully comprehend that good leadership is a byproduct of an integrative relationship between technical competence and human understanding. Success lies at the intersection of productivity and the heart-centered, emotional well-being of those solely responsible for delivering a product or service to a discerning public.

This book has taken me on an extraordinary journey of self-reflection. It has taught me that we don't live life for self-aggrandizement only. We can live a better experience, a life of enrichment because when we multiply the generosity of spirit, life is more joyful. We can live by the inverted pyramid model, the same as in business.

When we surrender our self-importance and allow people to have a more prominent role in our lives, we successfully reduce the gap between our self-assigned significance and other people's feelings of esteem. That is the gift of vulnerability. It is a three-dimensional offering for us and others because it allows us to be managed but not controlled while building bridges across intersectional lines—people taking care of people.

I have learned that we do for ourselves by empowering others. When people are empowered, they have choices. By permitting them to have a range of expressions, their ideas add depth, color, and texture to our dreams and desires. We unblur the boundaries which isolate us from each other by leading every interaction knowing people are imperfect. Everyone needs a little forgiveness now and then. By seeking ways to be caring and supportive and seeing the world with an open mind and an open heart, we allow the people within the horizontal layers of life to add value to our existence.

I like to say that the most potent authority a manager or leader has is the power they never have to use. Managers fail people when they believe they are more important than everyone else. They fail when they don't understand that the purpose is more significant than they are. They fail when they forget there is a difference between raw productivity and efficiency generated through acceptable behavioral practices. They fail when they don't remember that even the best managers are to the logistical maneuvering of time, money, and quality as real leaders are to relationships. And they fail when they don't read contextual clues to help navigate emotions better. In the end, the leader is not necessarily the person with authority. They are the person in the room that no one wants to disappoint.

Our industry has its fair share of great successes. We build superbly entertaining venues. We develop processes and systems that allow us to pass hundreds of people through revolving doors while serving countless meals with precision. What we don't do well is to teach the golden rule that trust must always precede performance.

Good managers and leaders have highly protective instincts. Their natural inclination is to create a force field around valuable employees. They act as human shields as they absorb, deflect, and keep unnecessary disturbances away from their team, knowing they are making lives more comfortable by removing obstacles. The safety buffer they provide allows creativity, communication, and free expression to flow, leading to higher productivity.

The notion of psychological shelter is not a new theory. It is part of the horizontal model of management where the boss leverages everyone's skills and is more closely aligned and in step with their employees' worries, hot buttons, and quirks. This promotes a climate of mutual comfort and protection. One human being saving another. While good managers have the mind of a mechanic, it is an effective leader who has the heart of a poet and broad wings, able to unite different minds in pursuit of a shared mission and vision.

Ultimately, this book became a search for mindfulness and my attempt to master the virtue of calmness. By focusing on recognizing where my emotions are taking me in real-time, I know how my actions and reactions lead to more positive interactions with people. Nevertheless, there is always more to do because natural biases get in the way. Circumstances and conditions change rapidly. Along the way, we make mistakes, some more regretful than others. But we can help heal ourselves by knowing our errors of omission, making us less likely to repeat them.

Being mindful of our feelings is a liberating experience. It is the eureka moment of self-disclosure that takes us to a place of authenticity less disrupted by raw passion or excitement, free of the constraints of the swollen ego. It is the sharp realization that we know where we stand in the moment with full-time clarity of purpose. It embraces a mindset of humility that transcends personal interests—one that creates a feeling of belonging because it brings contrasting perspectives together.

We can never stop learning about how our words and actions affect other people. It requires a transformation of the ego, which has been telling us for years how remarkable we think we are. Mindfulness changes the heart, and our behavior, by showing us how important other people are. It takes us to a place much less *dangerously normal.*

Glossary of Terms

A

Awakening – An "Aha" moment of sudden awareness.

B

Barbarian – (1). A human being perceived to be uncivilized or primitive. (2). An unmindful boss or colleague.

C

Cerebral Cortex – The thinking, rational part of our brain that barbarians never use enough of.

Character – The self-evident part of our persona which signals to the world that we have managed to sort out all our negative dispositions.

Cognitive Empathy – A higher form of empathy whereby the thinking brain is engaged in the process of empathy to form greater identity and sense of purpose.

Constructive Disruption – Used interchangeably with constructive discontent, it is the act of responsibly and productively challenging conventionally accepted templates of behavior and operation.

D

Dangerously Normal – Used to describe something detestable but is accepted as usual and customary.

Diffusion of Responsibility – Usually describes indecision or inaction in a group setting whereby individuals assume someone else is taking necessary action.

E

Ego – The "I" of who we are as individuals. The thinking, feeling, and willing self of a person that distinguishes them from all others.

I

Internalization – An idea or concept that moves from outside the mind and, through socialization, proceeds to a place inside of it and accepts the new norm as a personal viewpoint.

L

Limbic System – The subconscious part of the human brain responsible for emotion, motivation, and memory.

M

Machiavellian – A conniving barbarian with the additional character traits of emotional and intellectual dishonesty.

Mirror Neurons – Specialized cells in the brain which when activated provide a shared understanding of the needs and experiences of others.

P

Persona – As defined by Carl Jung, the "mask" we wear to effectively present our character to the world.

Perspective – The elevation of knowledge and a deeper insight, born out of the realities of experience.

S

Shadow Self – The hidden place in humans that holds the thoughts and deeds they would prefer not to reveal to the world.

Sincere Ignorance – When well-meaning passion and good intentions for a subject exceed education of the facts regarding it.

Situational Management – An adaptive or "elastic" leadership style characterized by the ability to flex emotional muscle to fit a variety of situations without losing authenticity or identity.

Soul Work – A deep introspection resulting in an awakening of the heart; an essential prerequisite to managing relationships.

Star Chamber – A kangaroo court-like atmosphere created by workplace barbarians to interrogate, berate, and tear down fellow employees.

Stealth Warrior – A special barbarian characterized by a dangerous level of insecurity who acts secretively to discredit someone they perceive as a threat.

T

Tor-mentor- An erratic and unpredictable barbarian who stretches behavioral boundaries by straddling a line between benign mentor and harsh overseer.

REFERENCES

CHAPTER 4: THE GOOD CHEF

i. Raymond A. Moody, Jr. MD, *Life After Life* (San Francisco: HarperOne; Anniversary, Special Edition, 2015), 36.

ii. Dr. Steven Taylor, *Out of The Darkness, From Turmoil to Transformation* (London: Hay House Publishing, 2011). 36.

iii. Ria Health Institute, *When Losing Weight Means Gaining a Drinking Problem.* https://riahealth.com/2019/06/27/alcoholism-aftergastric-bypass/36.

CHAPTER 5: MICHAEL AND THE STEALTH WARRIOR

iv. Dr. Gleb Tsipursky, *The Truth-Seeker's Handbook: A Science-Based Guide* (Columbus: International Insights Press, 2017), 44.

CHAPTER 6: FRED THE EVIL GENIUS, BUT WITH A SMALL "e"

v.   Daniel Goleman, *Leadership That Gets Results* (New York: Harvard Business Review Press, 2017), 51.

vi.   Rutgers School of Business, Leading and Managing a Multi-Generational Workforce. https://www.business. rutgers.edu/executive-education/ multi-generational-leadership/curriculum, 56

CHAPTER 7: TWELVE YEARS AND BEGGING FOR GRACE

vii.   Harvard Health Publishing, *Mental Health in the Workplace.* https://www.health.harvard.edu/newsletter_article/mental-health-problems-in-the-workplace, 58.

viii.   Center for Workplace Mental Health, Anxiety Disorders. http://workplacementalhealth.org/Mental-Health-Topics/Anxiety-Disorders, 59.

ix.   Integrated Institute of *Benefits, IBI Benchmarking Analytics Series: Short and Long-Term Disability Outcomes for Mental and Behavioral Health Claims.* https://www.ibiweb.org/short-and-long-term-disabilityoutcomes-for-mental-and-behavioral-health-claims/66.

CHAPTER 10: RECKONING ON A ROOFTOP

x.   David DiSalvo, *Brain Changer: How Harnessing Your Brain's Power to Adapt Can Change Your Life*, (Dallas: BenBella Books, 2013), 84

xi.   Tove Danovich, *In an Industry Rife with Substance Abuse, Restaurant Workers Help Their Own*, 2018.

https://www.npr.org/sections/
thesalt/2018/01/16/577462426/restaurant-industry-
workers-help-each-other-rise-above-substance-abuse, 89.

CHAPTER 11: RONALD THE SLOTHFUL

xii.   Dr. Neel Burton, *Hide and Seek: The Psychology of Self-Deception* (Oxfordshire, UK: Acheron Press, 2019), 94.

CHAPTER 14: HENRY AND THE HIGH PRICE OF PRODIGY

xiii.   Kerry A. Bunker, et.al, *The Young and the Clueless, Harvard Business Review,* December 2002. https://hbr.org/2002/12/the-young-and-the-clueless, 114.

CHAPTER 15: DREAM CHASER, P.F.C.

xiv.   Dr. Lawrence R. Samuel, *The American Dream: A Cultural History* (Syracuse University Press, 2012), 118.

CHAPTER 16: SAVING ANGELS

xv.   Beliefnet, *Seven Signs You May Be an Angel on Earth* https://www.beliefnet.com/inspiration/angels/galleries/7-signs-you-may-be-an-angel-on-earth.aspx, 126.

CHAPTER 17: OUR EMOTIONAL TOOLBOX

xvi.   Dr. Jay Lombard, *The Mind of God: Neuroscience, Faith, And A Search for The Soul* (Nevada City, Harmony Publishing 2017), 129.

xvii.   Robert K. Greenleaf. *The Servant as Leader* (South Orange: The Greenleaf Center for Servant Leadership, 2012), 134.

ACKNOWLEDGEMENTS

For my wife, Nancy - her heart is larger than life. She believes in all my hopes and dreams.

For my daughter, Sydney - my little miracle once smaller than a bag of sugar. She inspires and humbles me in ways I never imagined.

For mom - my beacon of light in the darkest of nights.

For dad - my Private First-Class hero soldier whose footprints I walk in every day.

For my editor, Jenny Watz - her respectfully direct honesty and thoughtful patience with a first-time writer was what I needed to keep going when I couldn't find all the words.

ABOUT THE AUTHOR

Jeffrey Sacchet is a senior hospitality professional. In his lengthy career, he has shifted seamlessly from renowned vertical hotel properties to famous large volume restaurants to Five Star boutique hotels to resorts and, finally, to private equity clubs.

He launched his career in a AAA Five Diamond hotel and learned the nuances and complexities of luxury hospitality at a young age. He highlighted his credentials at iconic properties, including New York's Waldorf Astoria, and then to the world's most celebrated restaurant, and one of its largest—Tavern On The Green, before relocating to another Five Star hotel, the Boston Harbor Hotel. In 1997, he was recruited to direct operations at the legendary 21 Club in New York City before settling in Florida in 2006.

He developed an interest in writing from his enthusiasm for learning and reading—mostly biographies and historical narratives—and his natural curiosity about the world and its multi-dimensional inhabitants.

This book was made possible because of Jeffrey's acute understanding of people and the driving forces of human behavior. He believes in the power of emotional fitness to manage the evolving and dramatic shifts in team member and customer requirements. Because of his many experiences and relationships with the industry's persistently complicated characters, he realized he had stories to tell and life lessons to share.

Jeffrey's passion is helping and leading people. He is also a certified career coach, assisting colleagues and clients to improve their brand while preparing for the next steps in their careers. As a teacher and mentor, he has developed dozens of future leaders.

Today, he resides in South Florida. He enjoys playing his guitar, watching old movies, riding a big motorcycle, and of course, he enjoys the ritual of dining with a fine bottle of wine.

CPSIA information can be obtained
at www.ICGtesting.com
Printed in the USA
LVHW111207110820
662878LV00007B/639

9 781977 229090